Katie Travels to

Victoria Falls and Okavango Delta.

CW01497349

Zambia, Zimbabwe, Botswana and Namibia

Catherine Black

Africa

My first view of the mighty Zambezi River is from the window of the plane as it approaches Livingston airport. Even the name Zambezi is synonymous with mystery and excitement. As I look down I can see the mighty river cutting its way through solid rock, separating the two countries of Zambia and Zimbabwe. Yes I am about to land in the country of Zambia. I am ninety-nine per cent sure that my choice of seat on the left hand side of the plane will give me an aerial view of the Victoria Falls as the aircraft begins its decent. I am tense with anxiety that I am on the correct side of the plane to view this wonder of the world from the air. This will probably be my only opportunity to do so. My attention is momentarily drawn from the vista by the pilot making an announcement. What is he saying? Simultaneously my eyes are drawn to white smoke-like clouds below, while my ears pick up the announcement saying that the passengers on the left hand side of the plane will see the Victoria Falls. What a sight! Wow, I can now see *Mosi-oa-Tunya*, the Smoke that Thunders.

Victoria Falls as the plane approaches the airport

As the plane hits the tarmac on the runway of Livingstone Airport Zambia I am still in a daze with what I have just seen. The short walk from aircraft to airport building reminds me that I have left the cold winter weather of Europe for the summer of the southern hemisphere. Today is the 1st January 2013. Happy New Year. What a way to begin a year. The immigration officers are already manning their desks and after completing the immigration form I am soon at the point of getting a visa to enter Zambia. I must remember at this juncture to ask for a double entry visa as my travels will take me out of Zambia to neighbouring Zimbabwe, Botswana and Namibia and then back again. This does sound exciting. Read on and I will share this exciting adventure with you. I hand over the completed immigration form with the $80 and after a few minutes my passport is returned to me bearing the full-page-size visa for the Republic of Zambia. I had read that immigration in Livingstone airport was slow and time consuming but today the plane I arrived on from Johannesburg was less than half full and I was sitting at the front so I was able to be first in the immigration queue.

It is only twenty minutes since I touched down in Zambia and I am now in the arrival hall of this small airport having collected my checked-in luggage. "What, she has luggage"? I hear my readers asking! If you have read any of my other books you will know that I only travel with hand luggage, so why do I have a suitcase containing 20kg of clothes with me on this trip?

I must change some money. It is the 1st January and the bank is closed but there is an ATM. Oh no! It is not working. What am I going to do as I need kwacha to pay for the entrance to the Zambian side of the Victoria Falls? I look around for an alternative place to change money but there is nowhere, so out I go to see if my taxi driver is waiting for me. I have booked the driver to take me round Livingstone then on to the Zambian side of the Victoria Falls then across the border to Zimbabwe. Will he be here? Two men in matching kaki shirts are heading my way and I can read the company name on their shirt pockets. I am in luck. Eugene, the boss, soon takes command and I am directed to a minivan which will be the mode of transport this side of the frontier. I have agreed to pay $70 for the afternoon. While doing this negotiation by email Eugene offered a guided tour of the falls for an extra $50. I declined this because I know that to see the falls a guide is not necessary. He introduces me to my driver and has another attempt at selling me his services as a guide. I explain firmly and politely that I do not require this service and I am soon on the short 4 km drive down Libala Drive from the airport to Livingstone town. As English is the official language in Zambia I have no problem communicating.

First stop in Livingstone is at the Jollyboys backpacker's hostel in Kanyanta road. No I am not staying here. I am only going to leave my 20 kilo case here. It contains t-shirts, underwear, dresses and jeans for kids ranging in size from four year old to fourteen year old. These items of clothing have been donated by the students of my language school in the town of Palamos in Spain for the children in the Lubasi Children's Home here in Livingstone. The Jollyboys hostel is active in getting travellers who stay with them to leave behind toothpaste and toiletries and any other items that they have which could be used by the orphans. I decided to take this a step further and bring some things for them.

The Jollyboys hostel is built round a little courtyard and the driver parks at the door of the reception. Eugene has the case out of the back of the minivan and is wheeling it over to the ladies at reception. I have not explained to him why I am here so I think he is a little intrigued. I have not told anyone what I am doing as I am still not sure if what I am doing is totally legal. I have not declared these goods as imported. According to my information I can bring in undeclared goods to the value of $150 but it is irrelevant as I didn't have to complete any kind of customs document asking what I was importing into the country.

When I explain to the driver what I am doing he thinks it is a great idea but I notice that boss Eugene has no opinion on the subject.

I leave the bag of clothes and we head back to the minivan. At this point Eugene asks for his $70 which I am happy to give him although I suspect that both he and I are breaking the law. It is now illegal to quote prices and pay for services in Zambia using any other currency than kwacha, but, given that I have no kwacha as the ATM was out of service, I have no other means of paying. The new law is not mentioned and I pay him in dollars and off he goes walking back to his office in Livingstone while we set off in the minivan.

Statue of David Livingstone in the town of Livingstone. Zambia

The town of Livingstone, named after the Scottish explorer David Livingstone who discovered the Victoria Falls, seems orderly and fairly modern. As we drive through a little park I see a statue of the famous man himself. Actually the whole idea of being in Livingstone town, Zambia is strange as only two days ago I was in Livingston town in Scotland. Now after travelling thousands of kilometres I am in a town of the same name. The driver stops so I can take a picture of the statue. I look up at this stone image of David Livingstone. Not for the first time in my travels, I am overwhelmed by the legacy this man has left. In so many places in Africa he represents such a big part of their history. Perhaps this is more significant to me because this Scotsman, whose ancestors were from the Island of Lismore on the west coast of Scotland, is an ancestor of my husband, a fact that my brother-in-law never lets me forget.

I am now getting a little anxious about my lack of the local currency, the kwacha, and remind the driver that I need to get some before I leave town. He is sure that I will be able to get money from the ATM in the Mosi-oa-Tuya Square shopping mall, so we drive there. Even though it is New Year's Day the car park is busy and many people are about. Sure enough the ATM is working and around it there is a buzz with the local people gathered in small groups looking at banknotes. What is the excitement about? Of course they are looking at the new bank notes which will be in use from today. The kwacha has been devalued and the new notes have three zeros less printed on them. I am usually verging on neurotic when withdrawing money from an ATM that nobody is near me and can watch what numbers I am introducing into the machine but today these friendly people around this ATM in Livingstone, Zambia just want a look at what the new notes are like. I get back in the taxi and the driver takes out the kwacha he has in his pocket and he too has a look at my new notes and compares them to the ones he has.

My drive through Livingstone tells me that it is a pleasant little town which would be nice to stay in overnight if I was not in such a hurry to see the Victoria Falls. During the years when Zimbabwe was not really recommended for tourists, Livingstone on the Zambian side of the Falls began to flourish. It has a good variety of accommodation ranging from backpacker hostels to fairly expensive lodges, and for anyone with more time than I have it is worth spending a couple of days here. From Livingstone there is also an exciting range of activities which can be done but for me I am now on my way to the Falls with the entrance money in new kwacha. It is not possible to pay the entrance fee in any other currency. It brings me out in a cold sweat just thinking about it. Imagine having come all this way to see something and not being able to go in because you have not got the correct currency to pay for it.

From Livingstone town to the Falls is eleven kilometres. This is where the town of Livingstone, not actually being at the Falls, loses out to its Zimbabwean counterpart Victoria Falls town which is actually at the Falls. I am now driving south down Mosi oa Tunya road. On either side of the road, on the fifteen-minute drive from town to the Falls entrance, are small shops and restaurants and soon I am passing the Protea Hotel where I considered staying the night. Now on my right is the entrance to the Zambezi Sun hotel and the Royal Livingstone hotel which are the two hotels on the Zambian side nearest to the Victoria Falls. Due to the high price for these two hotels they were never considered as a place to spend tonight even though from these two hotels you can walk to the Falls.

The driver is now turning right into the entrance for the Victoria Falls. On the right is the office where you have to buy the tickets. There are four or five people in front of me. One of these is a Japanese girl. I can see that she has dollars in her hand. Will they be accepted? Have I worried for nothing? The lady behind the glass explains to the girl that she can't pay using dollars. I have extra kwacha but I am not sure of the rate of exchange. I know I can change some money for her but this is not necessary as there are moneychangers who have suddenly appeared out of the woodwork, all willing to do a deal. Using my newly acquired kwacha notes I pay the entrance fee which seems to be 100 kwacha each. All the information I had, said the price was $40. Since getting money from the ATM I am not sure about the exact exchange rate but I think it must be about five kwacha to the dollar.

Clutching my precious entrance tickets, I go back to the minivan as it is possible for vehicles to drive another few yards nearer to the actual entrance to the Falls.

The car park is small and rather full but the driver finds a space. I agree to meet up with him again in an hour and leave my luggage in his van and off I go with only my camera, passport, credit card and money and a spare pair of undies in my small bag on my back. In all my planning of this holiday this part has been the most difficult to organise. If I want to see the Zambian side of the Falls before I go over to Zimbabwe I have two choices. One is to trust the taxi driver with my bag which has nothing of value in it, but, it would be rather inconvenient if I were left with no clothes other than what I am standing in, or take my 7kg rucksack with me on a tour of the Falls. I must admit that if this guy drives away with my belongings I am going to feel rather foolish. I would have preferred to have paid him at the end but because he is only the driver and boss man wanted his money on arrival at the airport I have little option but to trust him. This is strange coming from me because I trust nobody. I explain my concerns to the driver and apologise for taking his photo and a photo of his minivan showing the registration number. Well if I return and there is nobody waiting for me and I have to call the police at least I will have a description of the vehicle and driver as well as the name of the company that I reserved with.

I sign my name in the visitor's book and off I go along the path towards the Falls. Victoria Falls actually consists of five different cataracts, four of which I will visit tomorrow as they are in neighbouring Zimbabwe, and the Eastern Cataract, which is here in Zambia. I have read that the Zambian side of the Falls is not as spectacular as the Zimbabwean side and I also know that in January the water levels can be low so I am half-prepared not to be super impressed. After all, I have seen The Niagara Falls between Canada and the USA three times and have also visited Iguassu Falls on the frontier with Brazil and Argentina.

David Livingstone entrance to Victoria Falls

A few steps from the entrance and there he is again, a life size statue. This time I must have a photo of my husband with his famous ancestor. Just past the statue and I have my first view of the Victoria Falls. OK, David Livingstone saw them before me, but I wasn't even born in 1855 when he reached Mosi-oa-Tunya and renamed them after Queen Victoria. I don't much like the name Victoria Falls. I think that the original name Mosi-oa-Tunya, the name given to the falls by the Kololo tribe living in the area, has a nice ring to it and much more in keeping with what I am seeing now. I think that Victoria is a stupid name for this cascading body of water set in the middle of the African bush.

As a result of heavy rainfall in December, in the region which is feeding the Zambezi with water, I am seeing a water level in the Falls higher than normal in January. It is really spectacular. I am following the path to Knife Edge Bridge passing on the way some very wet people. Wow! Right in front of me is one of the seven natural wonders of the world. A few steps back I was beginning to suffer from being tired. I have now been travelling for thirty-two hours and have done three flights to get here but now all the tiredness leaves me and I have found a new lease of life. Perhaps it is due to the spray from the Falls which is soaking me. And I was worried that there would be little water in the river. I am really stuck for words to describe this body of cascading water, and on the slippery paths around Knife Edge Bridge I am really up close. This is exhilarating. It is battering all the senses. You really feel part of this. It is happening all around, the spray, the sound from the water and these beautiful rainbows which are dotted all over the place. The noise of the water thundering over the fault line into the valley below makes conversation difficult and being someone who wears glasses I can hardly see where I am going. The spray is falling like rain and the mosquito repellent which I previously applied to my face is washing off my skin and into and irritating my eyes. All the tissues that I am trying to wipe my face with are soaking wet and just disintegrating. But the sight of these Falls is spectacular.

Victoria Falls Zambia

I am now totally wet so there is no point in trying to do anything about it other than just accept it and enjoy what I have come to see. This is great fun. It is like being a child again. On Knife Edge Bridge as I look straight down on the bottom of the valley I am surprised to find that it is not at all scary. From here I have an excellent view of the eastern Cataracts and the main falls. Just look at that! It is not a rainbow but a rain circle. It is two rainbows which have made a circle and is reflected on the bridge.

Victoria Falls Bridge from Knife Edge Bridge

Spectacular rainbows

Walking along the path taking photographs at all the viewing points I notice a surprising absence of European tourists. All the people enjoying the visit seem to be from this part of the world.

Cascading water Victoria Falls Zambia

After about three quarters of an hour taking photos and watching the great Zambezi River leap wildly into a two kilometre wide abyss it is time to leave. From the falls to the car park is only about a 200 metre walk. It is only now that I begin to wonder if my taxi and change of clothes are still waiting for me in the car park. Oh, I do hope so, as I am wet, wet, wet. My vision is still somewhat impaired by the water trickles from my soaking wet hair onto my face and glasses. It is my husband who first spots the minivan and driver waiting patiently. Thank goodness for that, I would be feeling rather foolish if I was now telling you what I had to do to find my bag. In the car park are some stalls selling souvenirs but I think at this point I will resist the temptation to look. It is back in the minivan for the two minute drive to the border where I complete a departure card and I get stamped out of Zambia even though I only arrived here in this country two hours ago. But oh, what I have done in these two hours!

Zambezi River Gorge

Now I am about to do one of the highlights of this visit. I am now about to cross one of the most photographed bridges in the world, The Victoria Falls Bridge. It is of course the bridge over the Zambezi River which links the two countries of Zambia and Zimbabwe. I had a perfect view of it when standing on Knife Edge Bridge and now I am on it. Only two vehicles at a time are allowed on this bridge which is suspended 111 metres above the river. This bridge must be one of the biggest pieces of railway memorabilia outside of a museum and it is unlikely that it will ever be located to such a place. Cecil Rhodes, the instigator in building it, insisted that it had to be built where the spray from the falls fell on the trains crossing it. The bridge was therefore built below the Boiling Pot at right angles to the falls. The original steam trains puffing along this track were called *shongololos* meaning centipede in the local language. These trains must have been quite a sight. It saddens me to see these railways in so many parts of the world just disappearing.

Crossing Victoria Falls Bridge

The driver goes slowly but he is not allowed to stop on the bridge. After crossing the bridge it is out the taxi again and another immigration form to be completed. In my notes I have the price of the Zimbabwe entry visa as being $30 but it would seem that the price has risen to $55. Well I suppose I have no option but to pay it. My passport now is the proudly displays another full page visa this time for the Republic of Zimbabwe. Before going on this trip I had to get a new passport as I estimated that I would need about six blank pages to do the planned trip. I have already used two pages of my horrible new passport. I hate having a shiny new passport as it looks like you have never been anywhere. I like my passport when all the gold lettering on the cover has been worn away and the passport has a well used look. It looks like it's been somewhere not just lying in a drawer.

It is now time to say goodbye to my Zambian driver since he and his vehicle do not have the papers needed to cross into Zimbabwe. I take my rucksack and walk a few paces through what can only be described as an open-sided shed, give the piece of paper that I was given when I got the visa for Zimbabwe to a man sitting on a stool and head towards another man who is standing beside a car clearly waiting for me. He will take me from the frontier to my hotel in Victoria Falls Zimbabwe. This sounds very grand but if I didn't have a bag, if the temperature wasn't in the 30's and if I wasn't soaking wet I could perhaps walk.

Welcome to Kingdom Hotel Victoria Falls town Zimbabwe

After a three minute drive I am at the 294 room Kingdom Hotel Victoria Falls where I am to spend the first night of this trip in Africa. The hotel is sold as luxury but I am not expecting the standard I associate with the label "luxury". The girl at check-in is very friendly and very observant as she detects I have visited the falls en route to the hotel. Perhaps the fact that I am still soaking wet and standing in a puddle of water which has formed while waiting for the room key, gave her a clue. The hotel seems nice which I would expect given that I have paid £140 for a double room for one night. It is also very spread out, only being two storeys high, and I feel as if I have to walk miles to the room. Perhaps I am just impatient to go walking in Victoria Falls town. First things first, a change of clothing is called for then it is out into the streets of Victoria Falls. Yes, I am now in Zimbabwe. What is it like here? It is now after three o'clock in the afternoon and I have to do all my sightseeing here before it gets dark. Victoria Falls Town is safe during day light hours but after dark it is not recommended to venture far unless you know the area well.

Kingdom Hotel

I leave the hotel, walk through the petrol station as a short cut, and go up the main street Livingstone Way. I soon realise that it won't take long to explore this small town. On the left hand side, as I make my way to the shopping centre, are some small shops selling souvenirs. The painted fridge-magnets made from flattened bottle tops look like a good buy at $2 but I will look at some more shops. On this street are a couple of reasonable eating places but I know I will eat in the hotel. On the street are a number of groups of young men but they don't bother me. A little way up at the Phumula shopping centre I see internet advertised but when I get there I find it closed. The guard tells me there is another internet further in, in the hub of the centre. In I go but I don't really feel comfortable. It is not menacing but I just feel edgy here, however I stay long enough to catch up with my emails. The whole town seems to have more tourist police and guards than population. Remember that it is still only the first of January. I start to smile when I think that it is only four o'clock on the first of January 2013 and so far this year I have been in South Africa, Zambia and Zimbabwe. I hope this is an omen for the rest of the year.

Main Street Victoria Falls

Main Street Victoria falls

Carvings for sale

This is really a quaint little town. I suppose it is what is called a one horse town. On my left is a small field with little carvings displayed and an address where to go to buy them. Cutting through the town is the railway line which now goes nowhere but tourists can take a tour of the falls area on board a train using the line.

Souvenir shop Victoria falls Main Street

Dominating the town is a large park which today is being well used. It is full of children playing. The children are in small groups of two or three, some are running around but others are sitting in the shade under the branches of the bigger trees. At first glance this looks like a happy scene until I realise that there are no adults in the park at all. Are some of these children the street kids of Victoria Falls? They certainly look scruffy enough. Here in Zimbabwe there is the same problem as in Zambia. Kids, abandoned or orphaned who fall through the cracks in society, enter the cycle of deprivation and take to the street to survive. It breaks my heart just to think about the kind of lives these youngsters must have. If you come here to Victoria Falls there is a charity "Rose of Charity" needing the same help as Lubasi home in Livingstone.

Victoria Falls Hotel

Well, to explore Victoria Falls town didn't take too long. Perhaps now it is time for a look at the Victoria Falls hotel. This grand old lady is next door to the Kingdom Hotel. The Kingdom Hotel is at number 1 Mallet Drive and the Victoria Falls Hotel is a short walk up the road. Although it is nearly six o'clock the temperature is just about 28 degrees which makes walking pleasant. I am here in the rainy season and I do expect rain but obviously I hope I miss it. I can't afford to stay at the Victoria Falls Hotel but I can stretch to a drink. In through the hotel I go to the Stanley Terrace famous for serving typical English afternoon tea complete the scones and cakes. All the tables are occupied. At some tables people are still having tea and in the middle of the table is a three tier cake stand. I haven't seen one of these for years. I remember my mother having one many, many years ago. While I am not too impressed with this as a place for afternoon tea I have to admit that the view is stunning. Where else can you sip your tea accompanied by a cream scone and admire the spray from The Victoria Falls and also have a view of the spectacular bridge.

View of Falls from the garden of Victoria Falls Hotel

This colonial style hotel was built in 1904 when the railway reached here, and it is strange to think that until the 1960's this was the only hotel in the town of Victoria Falls, Southern Rhodesia. But now it is not, so I am going to go back to the Kingdom where I am staying and I hope I can have a quieter drink there. Before I leave I have a walk through the gardens and take some photographs. I am at first confused at why they have a stone plaque in the garden telling the distances to Cape Town and Cairo; but of course, this is connected to the railway. At the end of the nineteenth century during colonial rule it was Cecil Rhodes' dream to have a railway line which would go from Cairo in the north all the way to Cape Town in the south of the continent. What a wonderful idea. If this line existed it would be a sure have-to-do for me, but like many good ideas it never happened. This is a great pity. Can you imagine going from Cairo, up the Nile, through Sudan, perhaps Kenya, Tanzania, Zambia and Zimbabwe and Botswana then south to the Cape. I am getting so excited just visualising it. I love trains and this would be an incredible journey. Oh, dream on Catherine. It didn't happen and it won't in the future. The opportunity to build this route has passed. Cecil Rhodes' vision had many obstacles: geography, climate and interference from France, Portugal and Germany the other colonial powers. After the First World War, Britain had the political muscle but not the finance. After the Second World War the national struggles of the African people began. The only time when this could have been achieved was in the years between the two world wars.

In Victoria Falls Hotel garden

Ten minutes later and I am back at the Kingdom Hotel. The entrance is actually quite impressive. I didn't notice this on arrival perhaps because I was watching my bag. These wonderful, larger-than-life-size, metal warriors standing outside the main door give the place a very African feel.

Entrance to Kingdom Hotel

The foyer also has massive African statues looming down on me making me feel very small indeed. This hotel is very spread out and to reach the garden, pool and bar you have to go down stairs but the gardens are very nice with a bar which has fewer people than its expensive neighbour. I am very hot and a nice refreshing drink is what is called for. I am not a fan of coca cola or beer, I ask what they have. The waiter knows that I want a ginger beer cocktail. I have only been in this country a few hours but have come to the conclusion that the workers in the service industry all know what I want better than I do. This not being the case and having picked up on the words, ginger beer, I order a straight ginger beer not the cocktail version. For my husband it is easy, he always tries the local beer where ever we are. It is interesting to find that in the southern part of the continent of Africa so many British foods and drinks are available. Pies of all kinds; chicken, mushroom and beef are sold in all supermarkets and snack places. And to my delight, ginger beer!

Garden Kingdom Hotel

I settle down to enjoy my nicely cooled can of ginger when I am attacked by a swarm of what look like wasps. They are not at all interested in my husband's beer; it is the sweetness of the ginger beer that is the attraction. I try to fight them off but to no avail. So much for my relaxing drink! It's back to the room which is on the second floor. There are no lifts to the rooms and it is quiet a distance to walk through the gardens and over a bridge to the sleeping accommodation. In the centre of the gardens is a pool, not the swimming pool. This small lake, the bar and the swimming pool form the centre piece which the hotel is built around. The architecture is supposed to resemble the city of Munhumutapa, the capital of an ancient civilisation in Zimbabwe. To reach my room I have to cross a wobbly wooden bridge which sometime in the near future will require some of the wooden boards renewed.

My room on the second floor has a balcony on which the sun is now shinning. I hope that my soaking wet jeans which I hung out before my exploration of the town are now dry. Tonight I am going to have an early dinner and it will be early to bed. I have missed out on a complete night's sleep to get here. Adrenalin is a great thing for keeping you going when in reality you should collapse in a heap.

Bedroom Kingdom Hotel

It is now 7.00 pm on Tuesday the 1st January. I left Edinburgh Airport yesterday at three o'clock, flew to London Heathrow where I changed planes and flew overnight to Johannesburg. As the year changed from 2012 to 2013 I was flying somewhere over the northern part of Africa. At home when planning this I thought this would be something special to bring in a new year at 30,000 feet. I was wrong. The plane was full. British Airways didn't do a special dinner and they didn't announce that it was New Year. They celebrated the arrival of the New Year at the time in the destination country, which of course was South African time. So at about twenty minutes past ten I was handed a glass of revolting warm champagne to toast in the coming year. This was just not as I had imagined it would be. I don't even think I wished my husband a happy New Year because it wasn't New Year for me. I just went to the toilet and poured the champagne down the loo. When New Year in my time zone arrived, my husband was quietly dozing away, I was listening to sound tracks from the Rolling Stones, whose music is not my favourite listening choice, but I was trying to distract myself from the fact that the fasten seatbelt sign was on and that the plane was being buffeted about like a paper kite. Happy New Year! Six hours fifty-five minutes more of turbulence and I arrived at Johannesburg airport where I had to wait in transit for four hours for the plane to Livingstone. I am not complaining about this. There is no direct way to fly to Victoria Falls. But it does make you tired.

The scanning of the bags on arrival at Jo'burg airport was a laugh. My bag and the bags of the woman in front of me ended up in a great heap. A boy who looked about fifteen years of age asked if I had a bottle of water in my bag. I answered in the affirmative and handed over a bottle of water to him. This seemed to keep him happy and I wasn't about to debate the point, as I still had in my bag two bottles of wine from the plane and another bottle of water. Johannesburg airport at that time of the morning was quiet so I found a row of seats where I slept for about two hours.

At ten fifteen it was time to look for the departure gate for the flight to Livingstone. Twenty minutes before my flight was a South African Airways flight to Livingstone. Time-wise this would be much better but the price was more expensive. Before boarding the bus taking me out to the plane I was asked to show a yellow fever card. I have a yellow fever certificate. The man checking the boarding passes explained that sometimes the Zambian immigration authorities ask that passengers coming from South Africa are in possession of this certificate and if a passenger arrives in Zambia without a yellow fever certificate the airline bringing in the passenger is liable for a large fine. This worker explained that the policy of Comair is that the fine has to be paid by the employee who did not check the passenger's papers correctly. I do not know if this is true but I have a yellow fever certificate so I can go.

This is now my second visit to Africa where the need to have or the not need to have a yellow fever certificate is an issue. There are no clear rules as to when you have to produce this but my advice to anyone travelling in this part of the world is check if you need the important document. While I am saying this it is not easy to do this as the law seems to change depending on the immigration officer or the day. Last year I visited Tanzania and Zanzibar. All the information I got stated that I did not need a yellow fever certificate to enter either of them. This fact was confirmed by the Tanzanian High Commission in London. Three days before flying out to Kilimanjaro Airport I found a document issued by the health authorities of Zanzibar saying that anyone coming from the mainland of Africa had to be in possession of a yellow fever certificate. What a panic. At the last minute I had to go to the hospital for tropical diseases in Barcelona and have this vaccination done. I was asked to produce the certificate on arrival in Zanzibar which made it worthwhile getting it. My advice is if you plan to travel extensively in Africa arm yourself with this piece of yellow card as sooner or later you will need it to enter some country and it is not something you can do on the spot. Previously some countries offered this vaccination at the point of entry but this has changed perhaps due to the fact that you need to have it ten days before it becomes effective. On my visit to Tanzania and Zanzibar the card let me into Zanzibar but I was not protected from Yellow Fever.

At exactly the scheduled time 11:00 am the Comair plane took off on the last part of my trip to Victoria Falls. I sat down on the left side of the plane. It was wonderful. They served lunch at eleven thirty. That was the solution to that problem. In my planning for today I didn't have time for lunch. I was served a very tasty couscous dish which would keep me going to dinner. At exactly 12:45 the plane touched down in Livingstone airport Zambia. What a busy day today has been! I really need to sleep.

Now sitting here over the border in Zimbabwe I realise that I would in fact have had time to visit the Lubasi children's home in Livingstone. My friends who know me well think that what I did today was a little out of character for me. I am not a big fan of charity work and I often question the merit in what is done to help people. I am not always convinced that what is given as help is really help, so why did I bring a case of clothes half way round the world for children I don't know? It was after reading blogs and the comments about the Jollyboys hostel in Livingstone. They ask for t-shirts, soap and basically anything that travellers going home don't need to take with them to be deposited in a special bin. All unwanted items are donated to the children in Lubasi. This struck me as a good idea and when looking for information on Livingstone the name of the home appeared again so I had a look at what work they were doing. I am also the grandmother of six fantastic grandchildren. Although these children live in Spain, Canada and Scotland they have one very important factor in common. They are extremely loved by their parents, enjoy the security of living in a family and have never gone hungry. Many children do not have that luxury. The Lubasi home offers a home to orphans and vulnerable children aged between five and ten living in the Livingstone area. One little boy in care had been living on the streets for four years before he was rescued. Livingstone with a population of 114,000 has the highest incidence of aids in Zambia. With 30% of adults HIV positive, death from aids result in a high number of orphans. Traditionally orphans in Zambian society are looked after by relatives but in reality many are unable to cope with the high number of orphans. 80% of Zambians live in extreme poverty on less than $1 a day. At Lubasi it costs about $3 a day to feed, clothe, house and educate each child. The staff work for very low wages looking after the resident kids. In 2011 it opened its doors to twenty-six Congolese children whose parents were imprisoned for illegally entering Zambia on route to Zimbabwe.

I think I have answered the question as to why this establishment got me thinking. So, in the months prior to going to Zambia the parents of the children in my language school in Palamos, Spain donated a variety of clothes which could be put to good use. I think that every orphanage in any part of the world could do with a little help but this one does survive on bits and pieces of donations. The Sun International Hotel group donates food and some local businesses give bread, buns and sour milk. I would like to think that we in Spain made some little girls happy by giving them pretty dresses to wear. For my part it was easy. British Airways took the 20 kg case in hold-luggage from Edinburgh airport right through to Livingstone. My plane today was on time, the driver I had reserved at the last minute was there to met me, I got my sightseeing of the Zambian side of the Falls done with no hiccups so with hindsight I would have had time to visit the kids, but I didn't know that for sure. My hotel for tonight is, as you know, in Zimbabwe. What if the plane had been late and I was rushing to cross the frontier before the border posts closed for the night. Also after my communication with the girl at the backpackers place I thought she would get a lot of satisfaction handing over the children's clothes to the kids. As this hostel does not accept children under twelve in their rooms they do not get many small sized things donated.

Today has been great. Getting from Livingstone Airport, with a stop on route to drop off the bag of clothes in the centre of town, then on to the Zambian side to see the falls, then crossing the bridge into Zimbabwe was not easy to organise in advance. There are many transfer companies who do pickups from the airport and deposit you on the Zimbabwe side. The price for all these transfers is per person in a group of four, so if you are only two you have to share or pay for four people. Also I accept that not a lot of visitors jump off a plane and go directly to visit the falls leaving their luggage in a taxi but if I hadn't done that I would have to buy another visa for either Zambia or Zimbabwe. Remember every time you cross the bridge you are leaving one country and entering another. Trying to do the Zambian side of the falls before going across would have been simpler if I could have squeezed in another day and spent a night in Livingstone and visited the Zambian side then the next day do the Zimbabwe side. Well I didn't have the luxury of the extra day and I have enjoyed the way I have done it. I have to confess that the success of this day has been down to the services of Eugene's company. At the end of the book there will be a list of email addresses for the companies who helped me put this trip together.

I am more tired than hungry but I suppose if I don't eat now I will wake up hungry during the night. The Kingdom hotel has a food court near the entrance. I noticed that there is a place doing pizzas and pasta so I think a takeaway pizza to eat curled up in bed sounds just perfect. This hotel has had some not so favourable comments about being a little Disney-like but I really like it except for the walking distance from my room to the main building. So it is along the corridor again, down the steps and over the wooden bridge to the main building. At the side of the bridge is a notice asking visitors to refrain from swimming in the lake as there is a possibility of coming face to face with a baby crocodile. While babies in general are cute one with so many teeth is less appealing.

The casino and food court is at the entrance to the hotel. The casino with its slot machines and tables are in the centre, and around are eating places and bars. Not all are open but the pizza place is. This hotel is supposed to be full but there are only a few couples eating. It is strange. Where are the people? A large pizza costs $16 and takes about ten minutes to prepare and I am soon retracing my steps through the garden and across the not too stable bridge. I have a look for movements in the lake but see or hear nothing that would suggest that the lake contains any wild life.

The biggest problem here is these tiny silent killers that I can see flying about. My skin is covered with Deet and I am wearing a long-sleeved blouse but these crafty insects always seem to find the spot that the spray has missed. Here the danger of catching malaria is high. Two days before coming I started taking anti-malaria tablets which is highly recommended but the most important thing is to try and not get bitten; easier said than done. This time of the day and dawn are the times when you are most likely to be bitten, as it is the time they come out in their hundreds. There are over five hundred million reported cases of malaria a year and between one and three million deaths a year from the disease. While these figures are for countries where the population is not educated about the dangers of the disease and where they can't afford the prophylactic drugs as prevention or cure, it is a staggering figure that makes you sit up and take notice. Not all mosquitos carry malaria, only the females which can be identified by their longer legs but I think it would be a little crazy to spend time trying to identify the sex of an attacking mosquito to see if a bite from him or her is malaria carrying. Sorry all male mosquitos you are in for the same treatment as the nasty females which is a swipe from my flip-flops.

One advantage of the warm evening is that on the long walk from the main building to my room my pizza hasn't lost any of its heat. Accompanied by wine courtesy of British Airway I settle down to enjoy my "typical Zimbabwean meal" here in the very heart of Africa.

After applying another layer of insect repellent to my skin, I get under the mosquito net. The smell from the lotion is over-powering. I don't know about the mosquitos but the smell of this stuff would put me off going near it. Poor Mary Livingstone, she might not have died of Malaria if she had slept under a net. The famous man did many wonderful things but his unfortunate wife was just one of many killed by this tiny seemingly harmless insect.

Wednesday 2nd January, Day two of my Adventure

It is just after five in the morning and a shaft of sunlight is streaming into the room through the break in the curtains. I am wide awake and totally refreshed after sleeping in my net tent. The view from the window is not exciting but it is different from home. I have in front of me the hotel garden where two bush animals are playing; behind the fence is the path which leads to Victoria Falls and behind that the African bush. One of the advantages of touring Africa is that the difference in time between European and African time is only two hours; Africa being only two hours ahead of GMT so there is no problem with jetlag. I don't usually get up at five but I don't usually go to bed at nine in the evening like I did yesterday. Today is another exciting, adventure packed day. This morning I will visit the Zimbabwean side of the falls which are said to be more impressive than the Zambian side that I saw yesterday. Will I find this to be the case? Then it's on the move to Botswana. I am really excited about visiting this country. I really can't explain why this country has caught my attention but I just have to go there.

But first things first, breakfast is included in the night price so I am going to begin the day with a breakfast in a top hotel. I am sure that in the town of Victoria Falls there are a number of cheaper accommodation alternatives but in the last three or four years of travelling I have decided to treat myself to a bit more of home comforts when visiting far-flung places. When I was younger where I slung my bag for the night was of little importance. The excitement was in where I was and what I had come to see. I have in my youth spent nights sleeping on the floor of a ferry, on an overnight bus or train or even on the floor of a bus station in New York. Now that I am in the age group of the over sixty's and have no intention of stopping my wonderfully planned escapes I am building into my trip a little more luxury. In my books I want to show that the independent traveller can explore many exotic places without having to be packaged in a group. Whether you stay in a cheap hostel or five star hotel is irrelevant. I sometimes stay in cheap hotels and sometimes in more expensive ones. It often depends on the situation of the hotel more than the category. It is because of the position of this hotel that I chose it not because of its stars. It is after all the nearest hotel to the falls.

Once again I am on the long walk to the restaurant. If you have a low rise hotel set in gardens it is unreasonable to complain about the distance between the rooms and the facilities. I know that, but it doesn't stop me wishing I didn't have so far to go, also I sometimes get a little confused by the layout of this hotel but not so I can't find the dining room. The buffet breakfast is good but the number of staff is a little off-putting. At the moment I can count eight people hovering around the vicinity of my table not actually doing anything but watching me. I have perfectly good table manners but this is just not the relaxing breakfast I had in mind. Before I am finished eating my toast the plate is removed from in front of me leaving the toast in my hand. I know that having breakfast this early I will be ready for a cup of coffee and a bun about eleven o'clock so I always have a store of little plastic bags with me to pick up something at breakfast for my mid-morning cuppa. I usually do this discreetly but here I am not going to be able to do this with eight or perhaps more pairs of eyes studying my every movement. I have no option but to openly put two buns in a plastic food bag ready to take away.

The check out time for this hotel is 10:00am. That is ridiculously early. I am going to ask if I can have the room till 11:00am. At reception the girl is so sorry but they are busy and I can't have the extra time. I explain that I want to visit the falls and on returning to the hotel I expect to be soaking wet and will need to change my clothes. She understands my problem but I have to be out by ten. I have learned from years of experience that you never take the first answer you are given if it isn't the one you are looking for. I repeat my request and just stand and wait. I think I am now making her feel a little uncomfortable. I will try my best smile and see if that is effective. If that fails I usually get aggressive. I have a practiced ability to go from a smile to a face not to be argued within a few seconds; all part of being a teacher. Oh the smile seems to be working. She is agreeing to 10:30. I take that as a yes and promise to try and be back for that time, knowing full well that it will be nearer eleven o'clock when she next sees me.

Path to the Falls

For my visit to the falls this morning I am going to be more organized. I am going to take a plastic cape and an umbrella to keep me dry and a facecloth to mop up my wet face. I am also going to wear trousers which will dry quickly, not jeans. From my room I can see the path which goes to the falls, I only have to find how to get out of the hotel grounds which have a high fence all around. The two guards standing in the garden head me in the direction of the gate in the fence. At the gate is another guard who needs to know my room number before he lets me out. The path is a hard dried mud lane with bushes down both sides. It is not difficult to imagine a lion separating the grass and crossing in front of me.

What a vivid imagination! In actual fact, on my five minute walk I see neither another person nor an animal. Just before where the railway track crosses the road, there is a fork in the path. Now do I go left or right? I am about to choose the right for no reason when my husband tells me to stop and listen. In the silence of the African bush I can hear "the thunder that roars". The sound is coming from in front of me and to the left. I think I now know which way to go. Over the railway line I go and facing me is the entrance to the Zimbabwe side of the Victoria Falls. On the right is the road leading to the frontier which is very near. This is of course the way I came yesterday.

Zimbabwe Border

Playing at the side of the road are two baboons. Today they are disinterested in me which is great because these animals are pests. The residents of Victoria Falls have to live with these wild animals sharing their foot paths, the bridge between Zambia and Zimbabwe and even the town with them. They are incredibly troublesome as they frequently try to hijack food from people. Their main targets are plastic carrier bags. The baboons even attack re-used bags which previously contained fruit or food because they can smell the food. In June 2011 an American slipped and fell to his death over the edge of the gorge while baboons were trying to take his plastic bag. These are wild animals and should be treated with respect. I know that if they approach me I must not show fear or panic and keep walking on with confidence. I must keep an eye on them but avoid prolonged direct eye contact with them as this can be seen a challenge or a threat. I am not carrying a bag and these two are so interested in each other that I will just take their photographs.

Frontier Zambia and Zimbabwe

Entrance to Victoria Falls Zimbabwean side

The entrance fee to the Zimbabwean side of the falls is twenty dollars. Zimbabwe has the American dollar as national currency so there is no need to worry about getting money changed here. When I pay the entrance fee I get a piece of paper similar to a till receipt, but no nice ticket to put in my souvenir book. On the Zambian side they give you a pretty entrance ticket which I unfortunately got soaking wet and all scrunched up. Just inside the entrance to the park on the right hand side is an attractive café but I go straight ahead to the falls. Will this be better than yesterday? I find it difficult to believe that. Yesterday was fantastic. Once again it is a very short walk to the water falls. Just a little to my left is Devil's Cataract with Cataract Island on the lip of the falls. This is the lowest point in the 1,690m wide falls. Looking at this I think that it is not much different from what I saw on the Zambian side yesterday. I have only been here ten minutes and I am soaking wet again. The spray is falling like rain. Here on the Zimbabwean side the path winds its way through the dense Rain Forest. On the circuit there are sixteen different viewing points. From The Devil's Cataract I walk to the main falls. Before actually getting there the noise is deafening. What is now in front of me is sensational. It is what I have come to see and I have spent many agonising hours wondering if I would actually be able to see it in the month of January. In all its glory is The Smoke That Thunders. This name given to the falls depicts exactly what I am seeing and hearing now. The rain water is running down my face but I suspect that it is being increased by tears of happiness.

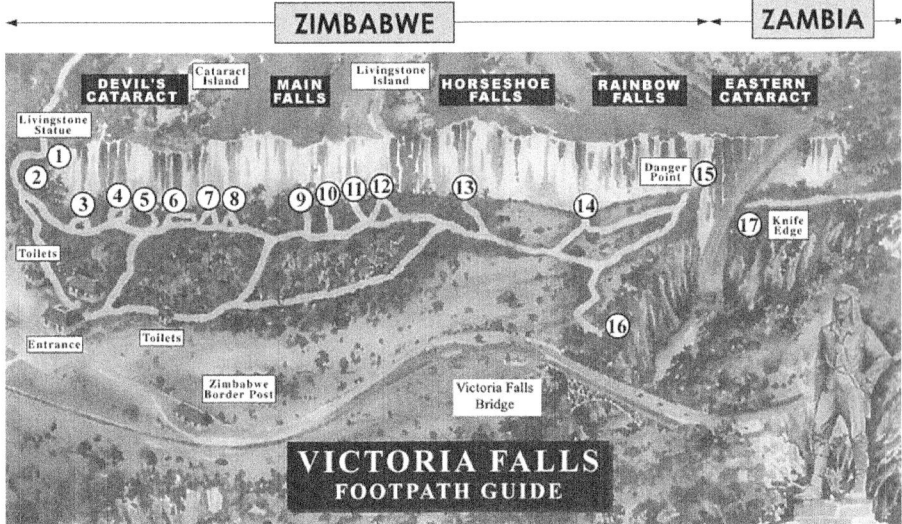

In the peak flood season this spray can reach 1km high and be seen from 30km away. At this time of the year between February and April there is so much spray that you can't do this walk on foot. At the peak flood time 550,000 cubic metres of water per minute crash to the foot of the falls. When you choose to visit here is very important. Sometimes there is too much water and at other points of the year there is too little. If I had come two months earlier there would have only been a trickle of water falling and some channels would actually have been dry.

Protective barrier!

I stand mesmerised by what I am seeing. This is something that you read about in a book and dream about seeing. This has been described as the largest curtain of water falling on the planet and I think it could be true. I stand and watch with the spray drenching me. My plastic cape is no protection. It is also difficult to get photographs and keep the camera dry. I continue the walk along the path through the rain forest. The sensation is that it is pouring of rain but there is not a cloud in the sky. From the Main Falls I continue to Horse Shoe falls and Rainbow falls and on to Danger Point. Is this better than the Zambian side? I have to answer yes, perhaps only because of the spray. But I do not think that any visitor here should choose only to visit one side. After all you have spent a lot of money and time to get here, so why only do half of it? Extra visas and an extra entry will cost about $100 in total but I think it is money well spent. If you chose to stay in Livingstone and want to visit the Zambian side get a double visa on arrival as this is about $20 cheaper than two separate visas and saves time. This is not a cheap trip. Actually the cost of visas alone is quite off-putting.

Close up of safety barrier!

The walk along the path is also a pleasant relaxing stroll through the rain forest albeit wet. One thing I have to comment on is the safety issue or I should say the lack of it. Perhaps this is the biggest difference between the two sides. In Zambia there are proper protection fences. If I were to have children in my party I would perhaps only do the Zambia side because I think it would be a nightmare watching them in the unprotected drops on the Zimbabwean side. In many places here there is nothing to stop you slipping on wet rocks and experiencing firsthand the depth of the drop. Fences on this side are only twigs and branches intertwined to make a flimsy barrier. A small child could flatten them. Doing the route at the same time as I am is a girl on her own. From time to time I take photographs of her and she of us, but many times she is taking photographs of herself. She has a tripod and is setting the camera pointing at the falls and then moving into the picture. As she does this she is looking at the camera in front of her and moving backwards to be in her picture. I think she has total disregard for how near the edge she is.

Please do not take one more step nearer

Walking on in the direction of Zambia the poor quality barriers stop and now there is nothing between me and the lip of the precipice but big slippery rocks. It really wouldn't be difficult to fall to your death here.

I have two ways of returning to the entrance. I can retrace my steps or cut through the rain forest at Horseshoe Falls. I am going back the way I came for another look. I am as wet as yesterday but the face clothe is very useful for drying my face. At Horseshoe Falls I can see Livingstone Island. This is where David Livingstone is said to have first seen the falls and had his hopes of a navigable Zambezi dashed. He was looking for a route from the interior to the coast. His vision was to establish routes for legitimate trade and so help in the abolition of the slave trade which he described as "this open sore upon the world". He must have felt totally deflated the day he saw the falls. The Zambezi River is the fourth longest river in Africa and the largest flowing east into the Indian Ocean. From its insignificant source as a small stream in the district of Mwinilunga in North West Zambia, close to the border where Zambia, Angola and the Congo meet, it travels 2,574 to its mouth in Mozambique, passing on its way Zimbabwe and Namibia. This was certainly what he was looking for, but without the cataracts.

The hissing, roaring, rumbling and crashing tell me I am approaching the Main Falls again and I soon see the clouds billowing from the cauldron. I am so very happy to have witnessed this wonder of the world. I think I could stand here all day just getting wet. I am content to just look at Livingstone Island but I know for the adventurous there are many activities that you can do around here.

After about two hour of walking in the "rain" it is time to leave this park. My original plan was to walk to the falls and take a taxi back to the hotel but the distance is so short and the path such a pleasant walk that I am going to return via the path. At the entrance are two or three stalls selling souvenirs so I have a quick look. I like a bag and ask the price but it is too expensive. I offer less but the guy with the stall is not interested. I can't believe the apathy of these stallholders. I also ask the price of the fridge magnets made from flattened coca cola. These are five dollars and are exactly the same as the ones for sale at two dollars in the shop in the main street in Victoria Falls. Obviously I don't buy anything.

As I am leaving I stop to chat with a couple who are about to enter the park. The girl asks about buying a cape or some protection from the spray. She is looking at my hair which is limp and has water still dripping from it. When I look at her locks I realise her problem. Her hair is a work of art, all tiny pleats. It must have taken hour to do it. The stalls at the entrance sell plastic capes with hoods and she buys one but I thought her husband's comment was good. The shower caps provided in the bathroom in the hotel could be put to good use here. A brilliant idea but wouldn't look too good in the holiday snaps.

This is Africa

I cross the main road and the railway track and I am awarded with a wonderful African picture. In front of me is a woman walking along carrying a load on her head and some young boys just strolling by. It is so African. In the hedge row on my right are two policemen partly hidden by the bushes. What are they doing there? They just seem to be sitting there. Are they waiting for something to happen or are they taking a break out of the sun? At the fork in the path I know which way to take back to the hotel. A few steps up the path and I see three teenage boys walking towards me with a variety of things for sale in their hands. At first I am a little concerned because there are three of them and nobody else around. I explain that I have no money on me to buy anything but they tell me they don't want money they would prefer to exchange their goods for my t-shirt or umbrella. My umbrella seems to be the item that they most want. I can have two or three carved wooden animals for my umbrella. When they realise that I am not going to do business they turn to my husband and try to get him to exchange his boots for some of their works. Knowing that my husband is wearing the only pair of footwear he has brought to Africa I am beginning to feel a little sorry for these would be entrepreneurs. They are in no way menacing just some lads trying to survive. As a general rule people who are trying to sell you something present no danger. The people you have to be wary of are the guys with nothing to sell but their "knowledge and service", the smart lads trying to make a quick buck without dirtying their hands.

It is now twenty five minutes past ten and I have made it back to the room before the code in the room card is deactivated at the half hour. A quick shower, change of clothes, a cup of coffee with the bun from breakfast, all the wet clothes stored in the white plastic bin liner brought from home for the very purpose, white plastic bag shoved in the rucksack and it is off to check out. Made it by 10:45: not too bad. I now have half an hour to wait until I am off to Botswana. There is not much seating in the spacious hotel lobby and what there is is occupied by the other poor souls tufted out of their rooms at ten, so I go and spend thirty minutes in the garden at the pool. I am a little concerned about my state of health because I would usually be in the pool if I had thirty minutes to spare but for some unexplainably reason this morning I am quite content to just sit in the garden under the African sun.

The next part of my trip I have reserved with a company called Adventure Zone. They will collect me here at the hotel and drop me off at Chobe Safari Lodge in Botswana. This transfer was easy to arrange as there are many companies doing this route. They all seem to be the same all charging around $70 to $80 dollars for the two hour transfer.

I am sitting outside the Kingdom Hotel waiting for the minivan. It is quite busily. Many minivans and taxis are picking up passengers. I recognise many of the company names on the vans. I chose Adventure Zone at random and they are now about three minutes late. Wouldn't it be crazy if I have problems with the link where I had a choice of companies. Over behind the metal warriors at the entrance is a pretty Kigelia Pinnate, better known as the sausage tree. This tree is so African although it can be found in many countries I always associate it with Central Africa. It is so "jungley" with its long rope like stalks and large sausage shaped fruits. Some for these fruits are more than half a metre in length and weigh about six kilos. We don't often see its pretty dark red blossom as it is nocturnal.

Sausage tree in front of Kingdom Hotel

Kingdom Hotel Victoria Falls

Oh here comes my transport; another very good quality vehicle. I expected the minivans to be older but all the taxis and transfer vehicles are modern. I carefully lay out my only pair of trainers in the back and hope that they dry out a bit on the journey.

The road south through Zimbabwe to Kazungula in Botswana is long and straight and although it follows the Zambezi River, it is never in sight. To go to Botswana from this area there are two roads running parallel to each other with the Zambezi flowing between them. If you take the road from Livingstone in Zambia this involves crossing the Zambezi by boat in Kazungula to get into Botswana while the road on the Zimbabwe side from Victoria Falls avoids the river crossing. I really don't think there is much difference between the two roads. They both take the same time. At home I had thought that going with a Zimbabwean company the vehicle might not be too modern but this line of thinking was so wrong. The professional approach of the company, the standard of vehicle and the quality of road are high even by European standard. I wanted to take the Zimbabwean side to get more of a feel for the country, but this is not the case. We have passed three cars going in the opposite direction and been overtaken by one truck. The road could not be described as busy and there are no towns or villages on route. It is just a boring road.

Typical painted dog

The only thing of interest is a number of road signs alerting motorists to the presence of painted dogs. Could I be lucky and see one of these animals? These African Dogs used to reside in thirty –nine countries but in twenty-five of these the dog population has been wiped out. Now these animals can mainly be found in Tanzania, Zimbabwe, Botswana and South Africa. These African wild dogs whose ancestry can be traced back more than 40 million years are the most endangered carnivore in the world. Today only around 3,000 of these colourful dogs remain and about one sixth of the population are here in Zimbabwe. Zimbabwe is one of the last strongholds of the species thanks to its wilderness, and it is commitment to the conservation of this black, brown and white dog. It is placed in the "specially protected" category of animals. I think I am now passing the third sign warning me that these animals are about but there are none that I can see. Perhaps that is good as people are the biggest threat to the survival of these animals. Road kills, shootings and poaching for bush-meat, are responsible for most of their deaths.

Is that a building on my right? I do believe so. I am now in at the frontier at Kazungula. It is out of the minivan and a goodbye to Zimbabwe stamp in the passport. While in Zambia the person I kept thinking about was David Livingstone, in Zimbabwe it was Robert Mugabe. To see the full affects he has had on this country I know that I would need to visit Harare the capital and more less touristic places, but even in Victoria Falls the poverty is obvious. I can understand his desire to make the country free from white dominance but his way of trying to achieve this was just wrong. In 2000 his decision on forced land seizures was an ethical and economic disaster. To throw out the white land owners with nothing, to give the land to his cronies, was a big error. It did not help the average Zimbabwean. These new landowners had no idea how to run a farm and soon the tobacco and food exports slumped and the economy plunged into free-fall. People who had had jobs in agriculture found themselves out of work. As for the white land owners they were lucky I they were still alive. From guerrilla leader in 1970, when his raison d'être was fighting the white regime of Ian Smith, to holding free elections in 1979, independence in 1980 his time in office has certainly made front page news many times. Ask anyone for the names of African presidents and the list will be short but the name Mugabe is known to all. He has one thing which he can be proud of. Perhaps his only supreme achievement is Zimbabwe's education system. Zimbabwe has the highest literacy rate in Africa. 90% of the population are literate which I suppose is a great consolation when you haven't enough food to feed your family or sufficient money to buy the basics in life. Perhaps for this country it would have been more beneficial if this former teacher had remained a humble educator.

Welcome to Botswana

Here at the Zimbabwe Botswana border the drill is the same as between Zambia and Zimbabwe. You are dropped off, have to walk a little and be picked up by a vehicle from the other side. Now that I am in Botswana my taxi is a safari buggy. Botswana immigration for me should be easy as I don't need a visa as I am British. This is not the case for all nationalities. In I go and there are four people in front of me. The border post is manned by at least three people but only one of these seems to be actually working. One man is sitting at a computer with his back to me but he is too interested in what is on the screen to be bothered with the humdrum of immigration. European football is much more interesting. After waiting fifteen minutes I can feel a need to shout at him building up inside me. The four in front of me in the queue are obviously from a country which needs an entry visa and their entry is taking some time. I have tried the usual nervous cough, the shuffle of feet but to no avail. One must have patience in these situations. Just then a woman appears and opens the counter next to where the tourists are being attended to. She stamps the passports in one minute and I am officially in Botswana. Perhaps all border posts should be manned by women with no interest in football. On reflection perhaps the football fan was waiting for traffic in the other direction, people exiting Botswana. I will give him the benefit of the doubt. On the wall inside the border post I see a box on the wall containing condoms. This was something I was going to see in many places in Botswana, a free supply of protection.

Botswana has one of the highest rates of HIV in the world. Only the nearby kingdom of Swaziland has a higher rate. A decade ago there was a national crisis when aids was on the verge of decimating the adult population. Botswana was fairly quick to react to the problem and now Botswana provides free life saving aids drugs to almost all who need the treatment. It has one of the most comprehensive and effective HIV programmes in Africa. This was possible because the country is small, having a population of around two million. It is also rich in diamonds and got help from international departments.

The way to travel

It is now time to climb up into this safari buggy again. It is a short drive about 7kms from Kazungula to Kasane my base for tonight. Oh we are stopping again. Why? I have to get out and walk over a dirty rag which I imagine is impregnated with something to kill any bugs on the soles of my shoes, while the vehicle has to drive through a disinfectant bath. This is really a pointless exercise as I am wearing clean sandals. If I have infected footwear, it is the pair of trainers which are still drying out. I am really getting exercise today jumping in and out of this jeep. It is not of the design where the back door opens and a little step appears. No this buggy has to be entered and exited by standing on a ledge just above the wheel and jumping up or down.

Kazungula is much smaller and quieter than I expected. I had never heard of this remote border village until I started to investigate this holiday then one evening, just a week before I left home, I was watching a BBC programme called "Wild At Heart" which is about an English vet who works in South Africa. In this particular episode he and some friends were rescuing animals, which had fallen into the hands of poachers, from cages in the town of Kazungula. A small world isn't it?

The town of Kasane in the north-eastern corner of Botswana has a very open feel to it. The houses are one storey, shoe box in design with one small barred window. There is plenty open space between each building. It is a very small rural African town but is situated at an important junction. Here is the confluence of the Chobe River and the Zambezi and the four countries of Namibia, Zimbabwe, Zambia and Botswana meet.

It is also the gateway to some of the world's most spectacular game drives. Chobe national park which is known as "the elephant capital of Africa" has one of the highest concentrations of animals on the continent. Chobe is a great place to see wild life and is so accessible both by road and air. We have just past Chobe Marina Lodge and are now turning into the Chobe Safari Lodge. This is the last time I will have to negotiate scaling the side of this safari jeep.

The hotel looks nice and my room is ready. As I am shown up stairs in the main building I know that this is not what I reserved. I have chosen the cheapest type of room which is called a rondavel which is an African styled round hut set in the garden. In the room there is air-conditioning a luxury not provided in the rondavel. There is also a very nice balcony overlooking the river. This is exactly what I need to dry off my wet clothes from this morning. As I go to slide open the balcony door I see a notice on the glass which reads "do not open as the monkeys will enter the room". Oh great just when I thought I would solve that problem. The tiny irritation of not being able to use the balcony soon disappears when I am investigated by a troop of vervet monkeys. I always thought that people came to see animals but at the moment I am being scrutinized by five or six cheeky, black faced primates. They jump from the tree next to the balcony, on to the wall and then on to the roof. What a noise, chattering and jumping. I hope they don't do this too early in the morning.

A room with a view

I think I should go to reception and ask if I am in the right room. Most hotels if they upgrade you they make sure you know about their generous deed even if it is for their benefit not yours. I also don't want to get billed for this room. I have transferred a hundred dollars to reserve this hotel but I still owe the difference of $50 and I will be going on a safari which has to be added to the total bill so I don't want any unpleasant surprises when I go to check out.

At reception the lady explains that they are painting the rondavels so that is why they have moved me. I am fine with that. Now it is off to the excursion office which is only a few steps from the reception. Here I have to confirm my excursion which leaves at three o'clock. I am booked on a river safari cruise. I have been on a land safari several times but never on a river one, should be good.

It's back to the room to have something to eat. In this hotel I am eating- up the food I have in my bag. There are two reasons for this. According to the hotel information the dinner is buffet and I have read that the food is often covered with flies and insects so here I am self catering. I also take food with me on trips like this and I want to reduce the luggage I have before going on the small plane tomorrow. When you don't know exactly what you will find in eating places I find that some crisps, olives and cheese make a good meal. To some this will sound crazy but if you have things to eat from home you reduce the chances of catching food poisoning. If you do this on the first few days it can make a difference. Just ask anyone who has had a really bad stomach upset while travelling abroad.

The kettle is boiling and for lunch I am having cup a soup. As it is now about two o'clock I don't have time for much lunch.

The Chobe Lodge is situated on the Chobe River and the boat for the safari leaves from the hotel. At three exactly a man is at the quay collecting the tickets. The barge style boat is not big and has plastic chairs set round the outside of the deck. I am lucky to get one at the front. At the back is a makeshift bar and two separate toilets which I believe are very small and only to be used in an emergency. Just as we leaving it starts to rain. The guide at this point is explaining the use of the toilets and making a little welcoming speech. The rain is getting heavy and there is no protection as the sides of the boat are open. I have in my small day bag the plastic cape from this morning at the falls. Yes it was only this morning I was viewing the Victoria Falls in Zimbabwe and now I am on a river in Botswana. Having retrieved the piece of yellow plastic from my bag I attempt to put it on. This sounds simple enough but in reality it isn't. The wind catches it and the flimsy plastic is buffeted around in the breeze. After a few minutes battle with the plastic I get my head and arms through the relevant holes but have to hold on tightly to the flapping ends. It is at this point that I realise that the noise from my protective covering is drowning out the speech being made by the guide. Some of the other people have abandoned the prime location seating on the outer rim and are congregating in the drier, less windy centre of the boat. Is this to hear what is being said or is it just warmer there? I think about trying to remove the cape and remove the sound but it is actually cold. I am wearing a long sleeved blouse, not because I thought it would be cold but as a mosquito shield, jeans, socks and trainers and I am cold, so the offending object has to stay. I try to sit on the flapping ends and hold the other parts that are vibrating.

The boat makes a quick stop at where I think the park fees are paid. Very soon I get my first sighting of hippos, lots of them. The boat is travelling at a comfortable pace for viewing, and the navigator is skilled at turning the boat around so everyone can get a sighting. In the centre of the river is an island of marshland where lots of hippos are grazing and others are in the water at the edge. I have seen large numbers of hippos in the Ngorongoro Crater in Tanzania but these hippos are much closer. In the wet season this island becomes completely covered by water. The guide is explaining the history of this soggy island on my right which is situated in the River Chobe which separates the countries of Namibia and Botswana. In the past, about, the 1990's both countries claimed that it belonged to them. Namibia wanted it for farming and Botswana for conservation of animals. After much study it was decided that it belonged to Botswana. Namibia is very near just on the other bank of the river.

If the weather was nicer this would be great but everyone on this boat is cold. A few people have brought a jacket but the majority are dressed in t-shirts and some in shorts. One woman is sitting shivering wrapped up in a towel. There are two couples with small children who are all dressed in summer clothes. I find I am clock watching too much to say later that this was fantastic. Up the river we all go. What is that in the water? A crocodile!. The adults all return to the outer edge of the boat cameras in hand. The two young couples seem to have forgotten that they have toddlers with them and are more into their glasses of wine and animal viewing than supervising their children. The rail separating the people from the river is not high and I think it would not be difficult to fall in the water. I have to confess at this point that these young Dutch speaking South Africans are spoiling this trip for me. As a teacher and grandmother I am always aware of potentially dangerous situations. If these children were with me I would have a good hold on them.

Elephants on the bank of the river

I try to block out the kids and return to the big game hunt. It would be nice to see a lion making a kill but today there isn't even a lion. I am treated to a sighting of a herd of elephants. On the river bank in front of us are some fifteen elephants. I am not sure but I think that one has just given birth. There is a baby lying in a hole and a group of elephants are gathered around. One elephant keeps nudging the baby with her hind leg. She is trying to make it stand up. Last year in Sri Lanka I was fascinated watching a mother elephant, whose baby was stranded on a rock in a river, help the baby elephant get down. She guided her baby step by step using her trunk and back leg. This elephant is doing the same but trying to get the little one to stand up.

Hippos everywhere

Two and a half hours have passed and the boat is returning to the hotel, when it comes upon a lone hippo and offspring. The mother turns in the direction of the boat, opens her mouth revealing an enormous set of teeth and makes an unearthly roar. Poor thing she must be feeling threatened. On the journey back to the hotel we are joined by other crafts which have been on safari too. It is amazing how quickly the atmosphere can change. One moment you feel that it is only you and nature but it can quickly change to being part of a circus. The boat trip cost $32 plus about $17 in park fees. I think for a three hour safari trip this is not expensive. It is a pity that it is so cold.

View of hotel from river

As the boat ties up at the hotel I am dreaming about a hot cup of coffee, so it is back to the room. This is one of these occasions where a kettle in the room is fantastic. At this moment I do not want to go to a bar or coffee shop. Imagine being in Africa and needing a hot drink because you are so cold. When I look out the balcony window to the river I have just been sailing on, I am very disappointed to find that the monkeys are not there, but I suppose that means I can enjoy my coffee and favourite biscuits without being watched.

This hotel is very nice. It has had some criticism that it is not really a safari lodge as it is too big. I like it. You get what you pay for. I have spent $150 on a room only base. Breakfast is another $16 each and dinner is $32. This for me is expensive but for a safari lodge this is cheap. If this lodge had been full I would have to have gone down market because I couldn't afford to go to any other lodge.

It is now time to explore Kasane. It won't take me long. It is a very pleasant little town on the south side of the River Chobe. Next door to Chobe Safari lodge is a small shopping mall called Choppies. I take the short cut through the waste ground between the hotel and shops. I go through the alleyway, perhaps this way is not recommended after dark, and the supermarket is in front of me. First before I can do anything I need to get some pula the currency of Botswana. This is one big draw back in moving from one country to another, you never have the required currency. So my first stop is at the ATM. I must withdraw what I need to pay this hotel and money to pay the hotel tomorrow night. I am actually staying two nights in Botswana but in two different towns. Next stop is the internet. Because of the way I planned my arrival in Livingstone I have not brought a laptop with me. I couldn't decide if it was safe to leave it in a stranger's car and I didn't want to carry it to the falls and get it wet so the solution to the problem was just not to bring it. All the hotels I am staying in charge for internet access so it is cheaper to use an internet café out of the hotel.

Between the town of Kasane and the national parks there are no fences and I have read that it is possible to see a hippo or elephant strolling down this main street but today I am not so lucky.

In October 1975, Kasane this tiny African village hit the front pages of every newspaper in the world. It was here that Richard Burton remarried Elizabeth Taylor. The person officiating at the wedding was an African district commissioner from the Tswana Tribe. The paparazzi flocked in to cover the event and for a few days every man, woman and child in the world heard the name Kasane. What wonderful advertising for a new tourist industry.

Chobe, which was declared a national park in 1967, was the first in Botswana. The tourist industry is helping to diversify Botswana's economy from the traditional sources such as diamonds and beef and creates over 23,000 jobs and the government has a policy to promote tourism while protecting wildlife areas. I hope that does not change as the attraction here is the wilderness. It is a unique place with its unspoilt natural resources and to change it in any way would be criminal. Tourism in Botswana is not for the mass tourist market. It is special and expensive. While the government make it easy to get in, citizens of the UK, South Africa, the USA, commonwealth countries and most western European countries don't need a visa; the high cost of accommodation makes it for the well heeled tourists. Botswana is not a destination for the people on a tight a budget. Perhaps the exception to this is the number of South African people who come overland in their 4x4s. It is very popular and not super expensive if you camp and have your own vehicle, but this is not such an easy option for people coming from Europe. We must rely on tour companies to supply the transport as there is no public transport especially in the remote rural area which we want to see. My opinion is that here in Kasane the tourists are mainly South African and there are a lot of them. There are many more people here than in Victoria Falls.

So with some pula in hand I make my way back to the hotel to the souvenir shop. I tried to buy some postcards here earlier and pay with dollars but was told they only accepted pula. This time I should be successful. They have some really nice big animal postcards so I must get one for each of my grandchildren. My grandson requested a picture of a giraffe so I hope there is one. I am in luck and buy a postcard of a giraffe but I haven't seen one on my travels. I usually never buy a postcard of anything or place I haven't seen but today will have to be an exception.

It is getting dark now. It is amazing how 70 km further south is making a difference to the length of the day. It is now about seven in the evening and it isn't dark. This is a good time to visit the river bank and see if I spot any animals. This hotel is in four parts. The traditional main building where I have a room, the new Safari wing in the garden, the rondavels built in front of the new wing and the campsite. I go towards the rondavels. They are very attractive. There are three steps leading to a terrace, and the round structure has a beautiful thatched roof. They are very African with lots of character and I can understand why I chose to stay in one of them instead of in a standard hotel room. At the river I see a notice warning about the possibility of coming face to face with a crocodile or hippo. I like animals but have a healthy respect for wild animals so I don't stay too long. It is getting dark now and this is the time of day that the mosquitos come out. Here in Chobe I am still in a malaria zone.

As there is little to do or see now, I retreat to the safety of the room. Thanks to my monkey friends I haven't had the window open so the room should be mosquito free. On this trip I haven't worn perfume only Deet. I can't imagine what it is doing to my skin but I know that it had a very strange reaction with the plastic of my sandals. It has melted the white plastic and I have a plastic V shape on each foot. Earlier I sprayed my feet before going out because this is where I get bitten. Mosquitos always go for my feet and ankles but looking at the pattern on my feet I think this anti mosquito lotion must be killing my skin.

I make myself comfortable on the bed and read the hotel information book. It has the usual details but the safety advice makes me sit up and take notice. It says not to leave the room after dark as there is a high chance of meeting with a crocodile. At this point I am very happy that I am in the main building not in a rondavel. Imagine being in a little round hut unable to leave for fear of engaging with a large reptile. A shiver runs down my spine. I am a bit of a coward after dark. I always blame this on my bad eyesight but tonight this myopia might be an advantage if I have to go out. Perhaps it would be better not to see what is roaming in the vicinity.

In Kazungula village there is a farm breeding crocodiles where you can do a visit and see these predators at close range. This farm is open all year round and costs about thirty pula for an adult and twenty pula for a child. So if you need more crocodile time perhaps a visit here would be exciting and safer than wandering the gardens.

Today was another up at dawn day so at ten o'clock I am under the mosquito net. I hope I don't dream about crocodiles.

What is clattering, banging and thumping outside? I think there is a storm brewing as the tree in front of the terrace window is making loud swishing noises as it sways to and throw. I don't want to experience a typical African tropical rainstorm on the morning I am going in a small plane. Oh please don't let this be the case. I extricate myself from under the mosquito net, find my glasses and get up to pull back the curtains to have a look. Hello there. To my delight the sky is clear and three inquisitive faces are again looking in at me. The other members of the family are responsible for the movement in the tree. They are jumping around so much that I am sure the branches are going to snap. Each one of these silver grey animals weighs between five and six kilograms and every leap onto a thin branch of the tree causes it to vibrate. What a lovely wake up call. It beats a traditional alarm clock although I would have preferred another hour's sleep. I would just love to open the window and talk to them without the glass barrier between us. Can you imagine if I had to phone reception and ask for some help to get the monkeys out of the room? I can just see them jumping around the room, hiding under the mosquito net, playing with the teacups, swinging from the fan above the bed and throwing my belongings around the room like a game of ball. Oh, I am very tempted. They have left the tree and are on the overhang of the roof and I can only see their tails hanging down but even if I couldn't see the tails the banging and thumping would give me a clue to their whereabouts.

This is another occasion when it is great to have coffee making equipment in the room. My husband will sleep for another hour but now I am up I need a cup of coffee. I have in my rucksack a little kettle and coffee bags which are as essential on my travels as my underwear. I hate Nescafé so I always carry some coffee bags of good quality coffee with me. I need a decent cup of coffee to start the day. The aroma of coffee or perhaps it is the clinking of my cup and plate has woken up my husband which is good as I need his cooperation in packing the bags this morning.

Today I am flying to Maun with Air Botswana the national carrier. The hand luggage allowance is only 7 kg and I know that my bag weighs about nine so I will have to check it in. I have read that if the weather is bad or the plane is too heavy they have a habit or just leaving some, or all, of the hold luggage behind. For this reason I am filling the check in bag with clothes that I could live without. This is quite difficult as my luggage is down to the barebones anyway. I hate lugging around unnecessary baggage. When I pack I only take exactly what I need. I dislike strongly people who when packing say "I'll take this because I might need it". Surely you know what you are going to need. As I said my bag weighs only nine kilos so what is in it that I can pack in the hold bag? No that is not what I have to do. My rucksack is on wheels so it is too big to go inside the plane even if I get the weight down to 7kg. I have to get all the things I can't do without in my day bag and the overspill in my husband's bag. To do this he will have to put some of his belongings in my rucksack to be checked in. I hate mixing up my things like this but it has to be done. While repacking three or four inquisitive faces reappear at the window. I am here to view the wildlife so why do I feel in this room that it is the other way round. I am the one who is being watched.

The flight to Maun departs at 11:00 and I need to organise a taxi from here to the airport four kilometres away. I go to the activity centre and the girl tells me they do a free transfer. Why when hotels provide this wonderful service do they not tell the clients? I reserve for 9:30 as I only need to be at the airport an hour prior to the flight as this is national flight. Then I have a thought. When I reserved this flight on line it was scheduled for 11:00 but a few weeks later I received an email saying that the time had been brought forward to 10:00. Great I thought and organised my trip in Maun. The same day as I paid for the Maun trip, Air Botswana changed the flight time back to the original hour of eleven. A little inconvenient, but not a disaster, but it would be now if they have changed it again to the earlier hour and I don't know.

The girl in the centre is very understanding and phones the airport for me and I speak to someone in Air Botswana and they confirm that the flight is as said at 11:00. This may sound a bit over the top but this trip is a circular with no alternatives. There is only one flight today and if I don't get this flight there is not one tomorrow. To go by land will take two days through the national park or the route round the outside the park which is much longer. Please make this flight go on time. If it doesn't I will have to rethink the next few days and miss out on the day in Windhoek Namibia.

Sitting in this office, in Botswana, listening to the chirpy chatter passing between the two ladies working, I am reminded of the TV series based on the books by the Scottish author Alexander McCall. His famous books "The No 1 Ladies' Detective Agency' about a female detective and her female assistant are set in Botswana. I have watched this series and the two working in this office sound exactly like the characters on TV. If I close my eyes and just listen I could be in an episode of "The No 1 Detective Agency". I am horrified when I realise that I think that this must be Botswana because these lovely ladies are speaking with the same accent as the actresses on TV.

I say goodbye to my monkey friends and hit the road again. As arranged the free transfer takes me the four kilometres to the airport. Checking in hasn't started so I find a seat. Straight in front of me fixed to the wall is another box inviting me to take free condoms. I do get the feeling that this government is taking the problem seriously and doing something concrete to help the people. One thing is telling people to use protection but it is great to see how freely available these condoms are. These boxes are in very prominent places for all to see. Is this a plus or negative? It is not possible to be discrete in the middle of an airport arrival and departure area. I can visual me trying to be fast and discrete and hauling the contents of the box on the floor or even worse in my haste not to be noticed, pulling the box off the wall and it crashing to the floor guaranteeing everyone's attention.

There are only two check- in desks, one for Air Botswana and one for Wilderness air. This little airline does private and group flights to more remote lodges. I don't have long to wait for the desk to open. Does this mean that the flight is on time? I do hope so. I have only this afternoon and evening in Maun. I am a little bit nervous about this flight. I prefer Boeing

747s to small turbo planes. In the past I had such fear of these tiny planes that I just avoided them completely but I am happy to say I now fly in them. The change of chip happened after I had a student who was a pilot. This South American had spent many years flying small planes in Argentina. During the time he was having English classes with me I went on a real adventure to Panama, Venezuela, Colombia and Ecuador. I travelled many places by public transport and this man thought I was crazy. I remember him saying he would rather fly a turbo prop with only one engine than take a bus. Well if that is the attitude of the pilot perhaps I can try one. I now use these planes to avoid difficult terrain but I am not a great fan of them. At least this flight is short. It is only fifty minutes.

Great the flight is on time. A short walk across the runway, up the back stairs of this turbo propeller aircraft and in I go. Inside seems a little tight for space and the windows are so dirty that I am not going to see anything, which is a pity. This flight will go over Chobe National Park and a little of the Okavango Delta. This is why I am going to Maun. From Maun I am going to see the Okavango Delta, this incredible inland delta formed by the meandering Okavango River as it fans out into an uncharted maze of waterways until it is finally disappears in the sands of the Kalahari Desert, walk in the sand of the Kalahari Desert and do a trip on a traditional mokoro. What a lot to do in one afternoon. This little insect of a plane is now lifting itself off the runway, up through the cloud and I know that what is below is wonderful but I can't see anything.

The cabin crew is one girl who is now coming through the plane with a basket of packets of little snacks and small cartoons of fruit juice. This is quite nice as I didn't expect anything on this flight. The ticket was not expensive only £57, once again bought online, this time using Air Botswana's UK site.

Now I am back on terra firma I must say that I don't know why I was so nervous about this flight. It was a good flight with no turbulence and I am now on the tarmac in Maun. Once again there is a short walk from plane to the airport building. I am standing waiting for my bag when I am approached by a woman who is waiting for me. She is Judy and she is the boss of Dumela the agency who has organised my trip to the delta. She introduces me to her father Jack who is to be my guide and driver for this afternoon. Do I need to stop and have some lunch before heading out of Maun? Why waste time on eating. I have some crisps and cheese in my rucksack that Air Botswana was kind enough to bring on the same flight as me. All my careful repacking wasn't necessary. My bag and I have been reunited without any problems but I suppose there was no harm in being prudent.

This is one of the cutest airports I have been in. It is in the town centre and looks more like a factory building than an airport. If I had wanted to have lunch there is a nice restaurant right opposite the entrance, in a small modern shopping centre.

Once again my mode of transport is a safari jeep. Thankfully this vehicle is not nearly as high as the one from Kazungula to Chobe. In I get and we are on our way through the suburbs of Maun. The road is narrow but has a good asphalt surface.

Maun is the fifth largest town in Botswana and has a population of 55,780. It spreads along the Thamalakane River. It is the headquarters of safari companies who do trips into the bush, companies that arrange visits to the delta and air charter operators who arrange flights to the remote lodges. The dramatic surge in the number of tourists coming to Botswana in the 1980s brought equally dramatic changes to Maun. Although it is the centre of tourism in the region most tourists don't actually spend any time here.

That could have something to do with the fact that there is only one hotel in the centre, Cresta Riley's and it is expensive. I would have liked to be staying in this hotel as it is so much part of the history of Maun. Sometime around the 1920's Harry Riley built a rondavel next to his own. It was only big enough for one guest and poorly equipped. At a later date he joined the two huts and built a restaurant. This was the beginning of the hotel which became a bit of an institution rather than just a hotel.

I think in the early days the bar there was the focal point in this Wild West town. In the early years times were difficult here. The main industry was cattle ranching and the big problem was tsetse fly. It wasn't until this was eradicated between 1930 and 40s that the area began to thrive and develop.

This town, which is the launching pad for adventures into the bush or up the Okavango Delta, began its life as the tribal capital of the Batawana people as recently as 1915.

The modern buildings that are around the airport are now giving way to cinderblock homes many with tin roofs. These small shoe box styled houses have replaced many of the tradition rondavels but the more I move out of town in the direction of the bush I see some of these wonderful old, thatched dwellings. One I have just driven by has old tin drinks cans in the mud walls. I wonder why it has been built like this.

Maun is unlike anywhere I have been. It has the feel of a dusty frontier town with thousands of donkeys. They seem to be everywhere, grazing at the road side, walking across in front of traffic or just having a nap at the road side. They are not alone many have some goats for company. In the autumn of last year a British charity launched a programme to put reflective ear tags on five hundred donkeys with the intention of reducing the number of accidents at night caused by these animals. Here in Botswana ten per cent of road accidents are caused by domestic animals. In 2010 sixteen people died and about four hundred were injured in road accidents involving livestock. The owners of these donkeys are among the poorest in Botswana's society and have no option than to let the animals roam free in search of grazing in this dry parched land. Here in Maun it is estimated that there is one donkey for every two people. Where did they all come from? Two hundred years ago Maun was bush and wild trees with lots of big animals. If you look closely at the donkeys here they have an interesting feature on the legs near the feet. It is "zebra stripes" similar to Somali donkeys.

Having turned left I am now on a road of much poorer quality and after a short time the road disappears completely to be replaced by a sandy track. This journey along this sandy way is taking me deep into Africa's untouched interior, a scene of extraordinary natural beauty. The Okavango Delta is situated deep within the Kalahari basin and is often referred to the "jewel "of the Kalahari. That the Okavango exists at all seems remarkable.

Shaped like a fan this delta is fed from the waters in Angola. The water's flow, distribution and drainage patterns are continually changing principally due to tectonic activity underground. As an extension of Africa's Great Rift Valley, the Okavango is set within a geographically unstable area of faults and regularly experiences land movement, tremors and minor earthquakes. By the time the water reaches Maun at the delta's southern fringe its volume is a fraction of what it was. As little as two or three per cent reaches the Thamalakane River.

What great roads

On I go through the sand. There is actually no road just a track in the sand and frequently Jack leaves it as the sand at the side is easier to drive on. This is the summer here and this brings the rains. I have been really lucky so far. I have not experienced one of the heavy thunderstorms which are frequent in the afternoon and I hope there is no storm this afternoon when I am on the Okavango Delta. At this time of the year the dry desert is dotted with green shoots and the trees have new growth. The rains are brining life to this otherwise barren land.

The journey to Boro the mokoro station is about 25 km but with no real road it takes an hour. I am enjoying this drive and the bumps are not bad. The scenery is the same all the way, sand, sand and more sand. Just think I am in the Kalahari Desert. Who could possibly be bored? At the side of the track is a woman standing waiting. Obviously there is no public transport here. I have read that people in Africa think about short distances in days of travel rather than in hours. Unfortunately for her we are going in the opposite direction. She is hoping for a ride into town. I am now seeing the beginnings of a settlement. There are two or three rondavels on my left and I can see the river in front of me.

Local dwelling

Jack parks the jeep at the water's edge near some mekoros and I begin to think that this is a mistake. A couple of kids appear who are interested in the new arrivals. I am studying this boat that I am going on. Its sides look very short.

Husband Bob

Poler ready to go

At that moment a tall thin man wearing tattered shorts and a very old t-shirt appears and greets Jack like an old friend. He explains that today he has a traditional mokoro for the trip. This means that it is made of wood not fibreglass. This is great news an authentic mokoro, made from a hollowed out tree. He pushes the boat into the water and then remembers that he has no seats. He disappears and returns with the bucket parts of plastic chairs. I wonder what they are using the legs for. The seat and the back of the chairs are placed one behind the other, occupying the full width of the canoe. Now I get in. A change of plan is necessary as my husband can't get past the seat in the front to get in to the seat behind. The seat at the front is removed and my husband gets in and sits down then my half plastic chair is placed in front of him. I glance at my husband's face and he looks terrified. I am not feeling too confidents myself. This seemed like a good idea when sitting at home but now I can think of all the dangers that are involved in this trip. I tell myself that many tourists go on these but it does not calm me. The tall skinny poler, I didn't catch his name, gets on the stern and with the long pole pushes the dug-out tree trunk away from the side of the river. The craft wobbles and so does my nerve. Perhaps I will just get out now. I am really happy that I can't see my husband sitting behind me because I know if I am afraid in the water, he is terrified. This boat is not steady and could be easily over turned by an animal.

Let's Go

I am now being poled through a meandering stream covered by hundreds of water lilies. To my left is the buffalo fence. I am beginning to relax a little as the mokoro floats through the reed lined waterway. It is so quiet. The only sound is the occasional splash from the long pole as the poler propels the canoe through the waters of the Okavango Delta. The papyrus reeds float above the sandy river bed, roots dangling free in the water. The gap between the river bed and roots provides the perfect spot for crocodiles. On I float in this watery wonderland. I am actually beginning to enjoy it. The tranquillity is incredible and I am beginning to relax although my bottom is getting sore sitting on this half chair. I wriggle a bit to get comfortable and the whole canoe goes rocking about. I must learn to sit still as I don't want to rock the boat. Where am I going? Oh no, to the edge to look for crocodiles. Sitting in the mokoro about a foot from the level of the water I have no desire to come eye to eye with one of these toothy animals. Round the water's edge this piece of floating wood goes with the poler trying to spot crocs. Yes, I admit I am a coward but I can think of many more pleasurable ways of spending an afternoon. I am slightly consoled by the fact that I not going to be floating around this delta for three days. One trip from Maun is to spend two or more days going up the delta, seeing wild animals and camping rough, the total wilderness experience. Adventurers can do this in the months between May and October. I am really happy I can't do this now in January as it is the rainy season and the animals have migrated.

Okavango Delta

I am sure that when I get back to dry land I will be happy to say I have been on a mokoro, but at this moment I am just praying that there are no Nile crocodiles around. It's mid afternoon and that tends to be siesta time for them, I hope. About an hour has passed and I think I have done well on this canoe. On the base between my knees a puddle of water is gathering. Just before we left the shore I noticed that water was coming in through the floor. The bottom of the boat had been previously patched up but the water was coming in at the spot of the repair job. I pointed this out to the poler and his solution was to push a piece of wood into the side of the patch. It is obviously not totally successful. Having no desire to drown or be eaten by a crocodile in Botswana in the heart of Africa I break the silence and tell the poler to head back down the reedy channels. Now that I know I am on the way back I start to relax a little and enjoy the surroundings once more. I also know that if I stay longer on this canoe for another hour I am not going to experience anything different from in the first hour. That is unless the water floods the base of the boat completely and I have to swim back. I know that I haven't far to go now as I can see the buffalo fence again. I am not wearing a life vest which I think is very irresponsible. At the moment I know that I am in the category of tourist who has left all common sense behind just because I am on holiday.

The driver Jack is a little surprised to see me back so soon. I had left my book of short stories with him to read while I was being poled up stream and he isn't finished reading.

Now that the mokoro is at the side of the water the poler is having a look at his repair job that was less than successful. I feel sad that this canoe is letting in water as I appreciate the hard work that went into making it. First of all a large straight tree has to be found. It has to be strong and durable. The types of trees used are ebony, teak and kigela (the

59

sausage tree). The bark of the tree is removed before the trunk is dug out. This hollowing out is still sometimes done with controlled fires. It is easy to understand why modern mekoros are made from fibreglass.

Even though the mokoro used on my delta trip had a leak I am pleased to have been in a traditional mokoro not one of the modern ones used to transport tourists up the delta. He tells me his boat is quite safe and perhaps it is as he only uses it for fishing. When returning we passed two dead cat fish floating on the surface of the water, which seemed to bother the local man. When the tourists are not around the tribal people who live here survive on fishing, cutting reeds and collecting water lily bulbs. Water lily bulbs? What are they used for. The answer I get surprises me. They are eaten sometimes raw or sometimes roasted. The reeds are woven into baskets for use around the house, that doesn't surprise me.

The buffalo fence which comes right down to the water is another interesting part of Botswana's history. In 1970 the European Union stipulated the control of movement of wildlife into the areas used by beef herds. This was to control diseases such as foot and mouth. At the time beef was Botswana's largest export and the government took action. They embarked on a policy of erecting fences called veterinary fences which were put up through some of the wildest terrain. These 1.5 metre high, high tensile steel wire fences stretch some 3,000km across the land. The idea was to separate buffalo from cattle. Unfortunately the government erected these barriers without studying the migration routes of the wild animals. Tens of thousands of animals died in two decades from denial of a route to water and fresh grazing. The best known of these fences is the fence I can see now. It is simply called the buffalo fence and it separates Maun from the delta. It was built to keep the buffalo and the cattle apart. The poler tells me that these fences are not all that successful as elephants can actually destroy them.

Happy children

Typical rondavel

I am now at the village where the poler and his family live. A group of kids come out of the rondavels to see what going on. I think this is because in the rainy season they don't get many visitors. I have come to see the delta and I am not concerned that the elephants, lions, zebras, cheetahs and other wild animals are absent. About 200,000 large mammals leave the delta area with the summer rains and make their way back as winter approaches. The absence of these animals means an absence of tourists so what I am seeing today is a much more natural delta life.

What a way to travel

Standing at the water's edge I am amazed that what I am seeing is the world famous inland delta of the Okavango at the point where it is swallowed up by dry desert sand. Nature never fails to impress.

A local passing

I wave bye-bye to the kids and wonder what it would be like to live up here in the delta in a round, one roomed mud house with a thatched roof. I am still thinking about this when we arrive at the spot where the woman was standing at the road side. She is still there. Jack stops and in she gets. She says nothing all the way back to Maun. Once again I don't pass another vehicle on the road until I am nearly at the main tarred road to the town of Maun.

Hotel in Maun Botswana

Tonight I am staying at the Sedia Hotel which is six kilometres outside Maun. The hotel is set a little back from the road. After leaving the tarred way and Jack has to manoeuvre his jeep around a little group of donkeys who don't seem to see any need for moving just because a vehicle wants to get by. Our passenger gets out and gives us a big smile but she still hasn't said a word.

Reception Sedia Hotel

The entrance to the Sedia Hotel is dull and the two girls at reception are not too friendly, but they are expecting me and the room is ready. At right angles to the main block of the hotel is a row of hotel rooms, motel style. I am in the first room so that is great I don't have a long walk to the room. The room is very dark even though it is only late afternoon. The room is naturally dark and the lights don't give out much light. Some of the lights don't work which doesn't help. I am only staying one night so I don't complain but there is no mosquito net. The girl showing me the room is one of the receptionists and when I ask about the mosquito net I am told to use insect repellent. In a region like this basic backpacker's accommodation supply nets but the Sedia obviously not. Here in Maun I didn't have a big choice of hotel as most lodges are further away in the bush or further up the delta, where tourists want to be. I on the other hand am only staying one night so I don't want to be far from the airport. The bed has crisp white laundered sheets but is home to a number of small black insects. I spray the bed with the cheaper spray insect repellent I have and nearly chock my husband to death. One good point about the room is that it has a fridge. This hotel room usually costs about 900 pula but I got it for 725 pula as I found the hotel on its old website where the prices hadn't been updated.

I have some time before darkness falls so I go walking through the grounds of the hotel. Between the hotel and the river is a big campsite which today has only three or four occupants. Although this hotel sells itself as having a riverside position there is a big fence separating the campsite from the river and the gate is padlocked. This is just so different from Chobe Safari Lodge where I was last night. Not being able to go to the river I think I will go to the swimming pool. I change into a swimming suit ready for a swim. Well not exactly. The water is a funny cloudy, greenish bluish colour. It is not very attractive. OK, idea number three, let's go to the bar.

The garden area while small is quite charming with the bar and dining area situated between the reception and swimming pool. It is not busy and there are two or three couples having a drink. Yes, I can have a glass of red wine for 20 pula less than £2. It is dusk now and a quiet drink on this terrace will be relaxing. It is great to get out of the dusty day clothes and into something dressier. Again it has to be long-sleeved, and my perfume has a distinct smell of Deet. The mosquitos are around but either the Deet is working or they just don't fancy me but either way I am left in peace to enjoy my drink. I read that the service here is very slow and you don't always get what you ordered so perhaps it would be recommendable to order dinner now. The waiter checks and double checks the order. If the wrong food comes it won't be his fault. The prices are reasonable, main courses are between 90 -110pula. On the menu is catfish and I notice my husband doesn't order it. Perhaps he remembers the dead fish floating on the surface of the river. Now that it is dark it is nice sitting here on this terrace with the bushes and plants decked in fairy lights, it is hard to believe that it is only the third of January and this year I have been in Four African countries. It is a typical warm African evening and I have no regrets about being here. I think about my friend I have left behind in very cold Scotland and know that most would enjoy sitting here with me.

The food only takes about forty minutes and I get what I ordered. The chicken is tough, the chips are very good and the salad I don't eat just in case, so dinner really is a plate of chips and another glass of wine. I am really enjoying this dinner. I know that sounds weird but it is a warm balmy night, the atmosphere is very relaxing as there are no loud people in the bar or dining area, and I am in Africa. I have really enjoyed today although I was a bit scared on the mokoro. Today was another day where my plans went well albeit thanks to the people here on the ground picking me up from the airport at the arranged time and taking me where I wanted to go.

It is bedtime and I am not looking forward to sharing it with my small, black, four legged friends. I spend some time removing everything that is crawling from the bed clothes; cover myself from top to toe in Deet repellent and in a few seconds I am out like a light.

Day 4 African bush to City

There are no African sounds to wake me this morning and I am relieved to see that whatever was crawling on the bed yesterday evening has not bitten me. The breakfast here in Sedia is much more basic than in the last two hotels that I have been in but the price of this hotel is cheaper. The breakfast room is small and in the main building near reception. As I am walking back from breakfast the strap of my plastic sandal snaps. It has rotted with the Deet I have been spraying on my feet. If this is what it is doing to my shoes, what is this stuff doing to my skin? Then there are the anti malaria pills that I am taking which are murder on the liver. I ask myself what am I doing to my body?

Today I am going to Namibia. Perhaps this is strange but going to Windhoek the capital of Namibia is solving a big problem for me. Today is Friday and I have a long haul BA tickets from Lusaka Zambia on Monday morning so I have to get from Maun here in Botswana to Lusaka Zambia before or on Sunday. I can't go back the way I have come as there isn't an Air Botswana flight, and I don't actually want to. I could go back to Johannesburg and from there fly to Lusaka. I also don't want to go that route. So when I found the flight from Maun to Lusaka with Air Namibia I was delighted. It is not the most direct way to go but for me it is the most exciting. I am going to Windhoek via Victoria Falls. Yes I know that is where I started this adventure but I can have another aerial view of the wonderful Zambezi River without the anxiety of will I see it or will I not, that was associated with the first visit. Then I go from Victoria Falls to Windhoek, stay the night and then go to Lusaka. This sounds odd but I can assure you that going this roundabout way is the solution. If I fly to Lusaka from Botswana by any other airline it is expensive and is via Gaborone or another city. If I fly back to Livingstone I will need to take a bus from there which will take four hours to reach Lusaka.

Sedia hotel also does a complementary airport transfer. As this is an international flight I would be better to get to the airport a couple of hours before. My flight leaves at 11:05 so at nine o'clock I am off again. The donkeys at the entrance are still here but this morning they are accompanied by a cow, and some goats. The cow which is really blocking the entrance is not in the least bothered by the fact that the driver can't join the main road. At first I think she is sitting on the soft sand at the entrance but then I see she is actually sitting on the asphalt of the road. I understand why it is so dangerous to drive here after dark.

It is only about ten minutes to the airport. It would have been less if we hadn't had to circumnavigate the cow. I am too early so it gives me an opportunity to look in the souvenir shop outside near the entrance. It has a nice range of African bead jewellery but no sandals. There are not too many international airports where you can walk out the main door and go to the shops. I think that the last place like this was in the Caribbean island of Tobago where I walked to the hotel from the international airport.

Maun Airport has a very relaxed, friendly, and prosperous but in retreat look. There is only one door used for both arrivals and departures. There is no conveyor belt for the bags; they are just carried to the door. Upstairs are some offices for charter flights and safari companies. There is a Budget Car Rental company, an exchange, and a ticket office for South African Airways. That's strange I don't see an office for Air Botswana. Although it only has one check-in desk it has a board announcing the incoming and departing flights. Today five flights are arriving and obviously departing. There is the flight I am on to Windhoek, two flights to Johannesburg one with South African Airways and the other with Air Botswana, a flight to Cape Town and one to Gaborone. This confirms what I found out at home. Going from Maun to Lusaka there is no easy direct route.

There is a departure tax for both national and international flights but I don't know if it is included in the price of the ticket. I look around to see where I can ask but there is no obvious place. I see a girl working in a back office and go and ask her. It would appear it is and she is the person who is going to check the tickets for the Air Namibia flight. I think there is a system operating here it is just not too obvious to me. I decide to change my pula into dollars and hope that the flight is on time. There is no shop or café in the airport so I can't spend it. At ten o'clock like she said the girl from the office comes and checks the tickets for the flight to Windhoek. Do I have any liquids over 100ml in my bag? No of course not only the body lotion and suntan cream which I stay quiet about. It is free seating not allocated seats. I imagine that is because some passengers will get off here, we will board, some passengers from Windhoek will disembark at Victoria Falls while some will get on there. I tried to buy tickets for this flight only going to Victoria Falls but this option was not available. This flight while going from Maun to Victoria Falls seems to only have passengers who are beginning or ending their journey in Windhoek.

My bag is now going through the scanner and I wonder if I will lose my precious suntan cream and body lotion. If I do it doesn't really matter as I have small bottles of both. I only got into this silly with big bottles because I checked in the bag to Livingstone with BA and took the bottles I had in Scotland. I lift my rucksack off the belt; nobody seems concerned about my 200ml of body lotion. I walk three steps to immigration, fill out another departure form and wait in the departure lounge.

This looks promising. Bang on time the Embraer arrives from Windhoek. It is unbelievable that these flights are on schedule. That is not a fair comment. Last year I was in Africa too in Tanzania and travelled around on an airline called Precision Air and the service was also good. I have been on a few Embraers recently and like them if there is no turbulence. This one is a thirty-seven seater. These planes make up the greater part of Air Namibia's fleet. I always think of Air Namibia as a big company but it actually has only two airbuses, two 737's and ten planes in total.

I am soon up in the air again. It was only yesterday that I flew into Maun. I really like moving about and seeing places rather than being in the same place for days but I don't very often have to catch a flight every day like on this trip. The flight to Victoria Falls is only about fifty minutes. I am now on the decent and I have once again a great view of the falls and the Zambezi River. The plane hits the runway and I am back in Zimbabwe. This time I don't leave the plane which is a relief as I don't want to pay for another visa. A few passengers get off and a larger number embark. It is raining quiet heavily now and I think how lucky I was only four days ago when I did my sightseeing here that it was dry.

Victoria Falls airport

The turnaround didn't take long and I am once again up in the African sky now heading for new territory, Namibia. This is a country I have had on my to do list for a long time and I know that one night in the capital Windhoek is not visiting the country but it will give me an introduction. I think that the interesting places in Namibia are far from Windhoek on the west coast so the next time I come to Namibia I will come from Cape town a city I have never been to, so to visit the capital this time will mean when I return at a later date I can concentrate on the Atlantic coast. I am looking forward to going to the city, after three days in rural villages. I am also going to stay in the Hilton. Yes I know that I am becoming a bit choosy in my choice of hotels. Actually I looked at the Hilton Windhoek when I started to plan my trip and dismissed it as being too expensive and had decided to stay in Protea Hotel as the price was cheaper. Then the Hilton had an offer and the difference between the two was only a few pounds so I am happy now that tonight I am going to pamper myself.

Namibia from the air

The plane is now flying over bush country as it approaches Windhoek airport. This airport is miles from the city and anywhere. It is a very nice day the sun is shining and I don't think it is windy. The wheels are down on the Embraer and I am only seconds from touching down. I can see the tarmac and can only be a few metres above it. At the point where I am expecting the bump telling me I am down, the left side of the plane rises sharply and the plane is at an angle. Where a second ago I was looking at runway, out of the same window I now see sky and from the other window the ground. As the plane wobbles out of control I wonder if I will have survived when it finally comes to a halt. All this happens in seconds and somehow up in the cockpit the pilot has righted the plane and with a thump it hits the ground on its wheels and bounces along the runway.

I don't want ever to repeat a landing like that. As the plane taxis to the terminal the pilot explains that at the point of touching the ground a gust of wind had caught the left engine raising the left side of the Embraer. Air Namibia only has ten planes in the fleet but it nearly only had nine.

Once again it is a little walk from the plane to the terminal. Nobody complains they are just so relieved that the pilot was able to correct problem. Oh, BA has just landed behind us and is taxiing to a halt beside the Embraer. What a difference in size between the giant Boeing 747 and the 37 seater I have just come off. I am really pleased that the two planes landed in the order they did as I have no desire to be at the end of the BA queue at immigration. Actually I am first in the queue but all the immigrations booths are unmanned. Where are the immigration officers? The snake of people behind me now goes all the way back to the entrance door and still there is nobody to let us pass immigration although we have been here a good ten to fifteen minutes. While scanning the building for any sign of life my husband spots one woman dressed in uniform proudly carrying a cake on a big tray, disappear into a room. Is it possible that there is a party going on and the passengers from two flights are having to wait to get their passports stamped? Eventually one unhappy looking woman comes to man one of the desks. I am first. I give her my passport. She says nothing then laughs and says she has made a mistake that she has put me as coming off the BA flight. Personally she can put me down as coming off any flight she likes as long as she lets me through to arrivals so I can see a bit of her country. She hands me back my passport so I can now enter Namibia.

The price difference between the Hilton and Protea Thuringerhof hotel was very little but there was a big different in the cost of the airport transfer. To take the transfer offered by Hilton was nearly double of that offered by Protea Hotel. Not knowing what the airport in Windhoek was like I did want to have a taxi waiting for me. Actually this is another change in the way I travel. When I was younger I would just arrive at any airport and get public transport if it was available, but now I try to make my life easier by having someone with my name on a board meet me. The absence of public transport in Africa also means that you have to travel by pre-arranged taxi service or negotiate a taxi on arrival. The difference in price is usually not that different so I prefer to have someone booked in advance to collect me. This time I got a receptionist in the Hilton to recommend a taxi. When I emailed Hilton and asked about a taxi company, the kind person who received my email passed it on to the taxi company and they contacted me. So easy. This is typical of what I have found on this trip. Everyone from hotel reception, travel companies and taxi drivers have been so dependable. Everybody is where they say they will be and do what has been decided in advance. I had meant to reconfirm this taxi but with Xmas and the festivities I didn't do it and now I am thinking I should have, but it is too late for thoughts like that.

This is the first airport in these travels that actually looks like an airport not just an air strip. It is not big but it is busy. I do not see anybody waiting for me so I am going to change some money into Namibian Dollars. Money in hand I go back to the door where I had entered the foyer, and saw a bench, with men sitting on it, facing the arriving passengers, and there is my taxi driver. Every situation has two sides to it. I am hoping that the taxi is here and the driver who hasn't been paid is hoping I am here too. He has come 40km to pick me up and it would have been unthinkable if I had gone off in another taxi. But I didn't.

The drive into the city is on a good two way road which every so often has a third lane for passing slow moving vehicles. The first part of the road is long and straight. I am now twenty kilometres from the airport and the airport lodge is sign posted. If you book this without really studying where it is you might get a surprise to find it so far from the airport. I never considered this hotel as I want to see the city so I don't know why I am concerned about it. Oh, a police check ahead. I think on every road journey on this trip I have been stopped at a police control. Fortunately they never take any time and I am soon on my way. This afternoon I am very conscious of the time. The flight from Maun landed at 14:05, half an hour to drive to Windhoek, the usual fifteen minutes at least to check in at the hotel and that leaves me with two and a half hours to see the city before it gets dark. If all goes to plan it should be enough. It is a pity that this airport is so far from the city centre. It is in the middle of nowhere. I know that this part of my travels is an extra. Never when I planned to visit Victoria Falls did I expect to be coming back via Windhoek in Namibia, so if I only have a short time here it is still a bonus. It still seems impossible that the easiest and certainly the cheapest way back to Lusaka is via Windhoek.

A few kilometres from the capital the scenery changes. I am now surrounded by low hills and the vast bush-lands have disappeared to be replaced by a green fertile valley. Now I understand why they built the airport where it is. Windhoek stands at 1,680m above sea level, in a basin between the Khoma Highlands to the west, Auas in the south and Eros Mountains in the north, 650 km from the Atlantic coast, at the epicentre of the country.

On the outskirts of Windhoek I drive through a very pretty, modern town not at all African in appearance. This is Klein Windhoek a suburb of the city. Downhill we drive and I am soon outside the Hilton Windhoek. It looks really nice all glass and shiny. I have certainly left the African bush and deserts behind.

Tomorrow I need to be back at the airport for the flight to Lusaka which departs at 9:15. Another early rise. Kleopas who picked me up at the airport is really friendly and a good driver so I see no point in organising somebody different for the trip if this driver can do it. Good all settled. He will come for me at 6:00.

The entrance to the hotel is a massive open space with a very high ceiling. This is my kind of hotel. Why go down market. Before leaving home when checking some details I saw on the website of Air Namibia that for the month of January if you flew with them and stayed at the Hilton Windhoek on producing your boarding passes at check-in you would be up graded at the hotel. At reception I say this to the woman behind the reception desk but she doesn't seem to know anything about this offer but she goes to find out. Meanwhile I search through the usual pieces of paper that have accumulated in my bag for the boarding pass. Back she comes and asks for the boarding passes without confirming if what I said was right or wrong. At this point I can't lay my hands on this piece of card 3cm x 5cms which is preventing me from having a posher room. I offer her a look at my airline ticket. Off she goes and photocopies it and then returns and tells me I am on the seventh floor, the executive suite with all the extras that come with being on this floor. Great, this is looking good but I haven't time to admire the hotel. It will have to wait till later.

Have you ever noticed that in real upmarket hotels you are left in peace to wheel your bag to the room all on your own? Sometimes I wonder how I manage to get my bag half way across the world when hotel staff seems to think I am unable to wheel it to a lift. Nobody shows you how to switch on the TV, where the bathroom is and how to open the mini bar. The room is fabulous, all super modern with one of these open plan bathrooms, big king bed topped with enough pillows to open a bedding shop and a wonderful view of the city. Ten minutes later the room doesn't look quite as good as I have tipped out my rucksack to find a change of clothes, put my money belt in the safe and had a drink of water. It now has a more lived in look.

Super modern Hilton

Down I go in the glass lift. I and not a fan of lifts especially the old creaky types but I adore these glass sided lifts that give you a great view of what is around. I could just about do my sightseeing of Windhoek from here.

Now I am on ground level it's out of the hotel, across a big car park and I am in Independence Avenue which is the main artery of this city. Two minutes from my room and I am where I want to be. The weather is perfect. This is the best weather I have had. Hot and sunny with a perfect blue sky and not a breathe of air. I am still wondering if the explanation for the wobble in the landing is true as it is not at all windy. Well I suppose I will never know and does it really matter.

Independence Avenue from Hilton Hotel

On my right is Zoo Park, a lovely green area in the centre. There is no zoo here it is just a park but I haven't time to sit in it. Up Independence Avenue I walk enjoying this modern city with its shopping malls leading off the main street. The shops are a mixture of souvenir shops, and the usual High street outlets. This city's shopping could be in any European Country. Perhaps the only clue to it being in Africa is the many items for sale that are made from animal skins. The architecture is very German as a result of its historic links with Germany. It is also very clean and orderly. Because of its cleanliness it is often pronounced the most un-African city in Africa. At the red clock tower I turn left and explore some of the side streets. Here are a number of restaurants, and outdoor cafes; a perfect place to watch the street life of Windhoek. The population of 250,000, which is growing rapidly due to unemployment in rural areas, is an ethnic mix and the language I hear spoken is English although there are local dialects too.

Gibeon Meteorites

I am now in Post Office Street and I know that at the end of this street is a supermarket in the Wernhill Centre. This would be a good place to stock up with drinks. At the end of Post Office Street are some strange looking stones mounted on steel columns. Ah these must be the Gibeon Meteorites from the small Namibian town of the same name. The display is very unusual and makes a stunning centre piece for the city.

Town centre Windhoek

All down Post Office Street are craft sellers with wire statues, beautiful vases and bowls made out of wood all displayed on the pavement. I could spend hours in this street if I had more time. I am tempted to stop and buy but I am not going to load up with things until I get to Lusaka. Lusaka is shopping, but one thing I do need is a pair of sandals. All the beautiful things made of skin and I can't find a pair of leather sandals. They all seem to be big sizes. In the end I buy a pair of flip flops which will do for going to the pool.

I now seldom wear sandals when sightseeing. This is to keep my husband happy. He was very unhappy in Myanmar when I wore flip flops all the time. In the capital Rangoon the raw sewage was floating in the street and I had to paddle through it. This was not the first time I had been in places where a cut or a bashed toe could result in a more serious illness, so I had to promise if I go to less salubrious places I have to wear trainers. It is a small price to pay for having my husband's company and actually he is right, although my favourite foot wear is flip flops. They are so practical, in the sun or rain, light to carry and of course very fashionable.

Kudu Windhoek

There is one thing I must see here in Windhoek and that is the bronze statue of the Kudu. Every picture or this city shows it. It is such a part of Windhoek that residents use it to give directions. So, it is back to Independence Avenue and continue up in the direction of the station. The more I go up Independence the poorer it gets. The shops are less glossy, the supermarkets are of less upmarket chains and there is a big change in the people. The tourists have mostly gone and the smart city dwellers are replaced by women shopping for food. The chic outdoor cafes are replaced by take away joints like The Hungry Lion.

I can now see the kudu statue, so not far to go. It is in Independence Avenue at the crossroads of John Meinhert Street. I cross the street for the usual snaps just to prove I have been in Windhoek. I am a little disappointed at the position of this famous land mark. If I had been talking I could have walked past it. I don't know what I was expecting. Perhaps that it was in a square or a park, not hidden at the side of the road. It is a small pretty statue of the animal but not special.

I am not going to go much further up Independence Avenue. I turn and head for the hotel but the smell of chips from the Hungry Lion makes me realise how hungry I am. Apart from what I had to eat on Air Namibia I have had no lunch and it is now quarter to five. No wonder the aroma of fried food is getting to me. Imagine being in Africa and having a bag of chips swimming in vinegar. Perhaps I should feel ashamed that I am eating such British fare here in the continent of Africa but it is so good.

The cars on Independence Avenue have reduced in number, but not in speed. This wide now half empty road is like a race track. The few remaining car are going at speeds unbelievable for a city centre. It is now nearly five o'clock and the shops are closing up. The street traders have all gone and the city is shutting down for the night. I am nearly back at the Hilton Hotel so I think that my trip to Windhoek is over. It was short but I have enjoyed it. I saw what I wanted to see and now I am going to relax and enjoy the Hilton.

I read that Windhoek has a high level of crime and that tourists are often targeted. Muggings are not exceptional and that you are as likely to be a victim of crime in the centre of the city as in a township. Perhaps that is the case but I never felt at any time uncomfortable while exploring. I know that most crime happens when you are in the wrong place at the wrong time, so perhaps today I was in the right place at the right time.

View from hotel window

One famous building I didn't go to visit was the Christ Church. The reason for not visiting it is that from the upper floors of the hotel I have the perfect view; actually I am lucky to see it from the bedroom window. Sitting on a traffic island, right in front of me is this German church, a landmark in this city. It is not a big flashy cathedral but a church in size proportional to the city. Built of sandstone with its 40m high spire this church competes with the kudu statue to be on every post card of Windhoek. The clock, the three bells and the stained glass windows all came from Germany.

Katutura, I am not sure if I should have made time for a short visit to this township of squatter camps and iron sheet, tin houses. I decided not to try as I have visited Soweto in Johannesburg and some poor shanty towns in South America. Every big city has the same structure, wealth in and around the centre while some less fortunate suburbs stink of poverty. Here in Africa these townships arose due to the apartheid system. Katutura was established in the 1950's when the black population was forced to relocate here, now 60% of the population of Windhoek live in Katutura or one of its suburbs. Tourists visit slum areas and I have to ask why. If they go to a market and buy that does inject some money into the pockets of the local people but just to visit! Perhaps it makes them feel better about what they have, where they live and the manner in which they live, but it doesn't help the local community. Hard though it may sound, in the majority of cases the people of these slums have to help themselves. This is the case in Dolam a township in Katutura where the crime rate is horrifying. Every weekend families here bury loved ones who have been stabbed or raped to death. Now this township is working with and cooperating with the police in an intensive attempt to improve the area.

I have seen perhaps one of the worst slums in Africa and if I close my eyes I can still smell it in my nostrils. While in Mombasa in Kenya I went through the area of the city where the Somalia refugees have made camp and that was horrendous. I really don't need to experience anything like it again.

Soweto was different. It is a history lesson in the fight for the rights of blacks to have some say in their country. Soweto is and will always be a township with the poverty that accompanies it, but with Nelson Mandela's house and the Hector Pieterson museum telling the story of the struggle against the brutality of the apartheid government, history of my generation comes alive. Well worth a visit but just to gloat at poverty for no reason is another issue. I have in the past been attracted to places where the standard of living is atrocious but now I question why I went.

Do I feel guilty about what I have in comparison? I don't think so. Inequality is something we live with every day of our lives. I read a comment from a girl in trip advisor which said she couldn't justify staying in a five star hotel when on the door step the people were living in such poverty so she stayed in a cheaper place. What difference did it make to the people she was so concerned about where she stayed unless she donated the difference in price to a needy cause. I continued reading and couldn't believe what came next. She had comments on the activities she had done, bungee jumping, elephant rides and a river cruise. I am sure she rubbed shoulder with the poor on all of these. The world is full of inequality that is the way it is and as visitors to any country we must be carefully what we do in our attempts to help. Having this view point is why I surprised my friends when I took with me on this trip the clothes for the children in the orphanage. I am not hard and unsympathetic. In Vietnam at the end of a week I could have sent a post card to everyone I have ever known. The people of Vietnam didn't want hand-outs, they wanted to work, even the kids. Every time I was asked to buy postcards from the street kids I couldn't say no. I hate people who ask for money, but I frequently give food to beggars and also enjoy five star hotels.

I am now in the room of the hotel and wish that I hadn't left it so untidy but I was in a hurry to go and visit the town. While the bath is filling up with hot water and bubbles I do a quick tidy up. I enjoy staying in a hotel of this category but it is spoiled if I have the room untidy. It is a real luxury to have a bath and after not have to cover every part of my skin with Deet. I can now also wear a short sleeved t-shirt and dress for the city not the bush. It is a pity I don't have a pair of sandals but my newly bought flip flops will have to do. I am now in a malaria free zone and I don't think I was bitten on my travels.

Windhoek

If you have the good fortune to be on the executive floor, you must use the facilities offered, after all that is what they are there for. It is into my glass lift again and up to the 12th floor. It is nearly seven o'clock and it isn't dark. The 12th floor, which has the roof terrace and open air bar, is beautiful. It has a long narrow pool down one side and booths and chairs for intimate meetings occupying the rest of the open-air space. The bar is up in the top corner. The views of Windhoek are stunning. If all these other people were not here it would be just perfect. I think I could find an empty chair but sure it wouldn't be where I want to sit. The bar is also very busy which is not really a problem. Good evening madam, are you looking for a table? Can you I imagine his face if I reply no thank you, this client in the five star hotel had a bag of chips on the street at half past four and isn't hungry now. No I am not "dinner" hungry but some nibbles would be nice, so along the side of the pool I walk and into the executive lounge. It is empty. What a difference from the outdoor terrace. This is a sanctuary. From the fridge I help myself to a small bottle of sparkling water and again my husband samples the local brew, this time Windhoek lager, the local beer. The view from inside is the same as from the terrace but it is possible to walk round and enjoy it free from other people. When I have seen all, I sit and relax and read the local newspaper. Two business men have now arrived and are attacking the food so if I am to eat perhaps this is the time. A glass of white wine and some samosas will do just nicely. I can also check in for the flight tomorrow morning. Having free access to a computer is also nice. I email all my family telling them my good luck in being upgraded. Is it good luck or is my being on the ball and spotting the offer. I say good night to the executive club steward who invites me for breakfast the next day but sadly I will have to pass on that invitation as I have another of my early starts.

Day 5 Back to Zambia

It is Saturday 5th January at six o'clock in the morning and Kleopas is already waiting to take me to the airport. The fifty minute drive is the same as yesterday and I arrive at the airport in good time. It is quite busy. As the plane is again an Embraer, I am going to check in my bag so I join the check-in queue for Air Namibia. It is nearly my turn when I notice that the bags around me have all got a yellow label tied to them. I ask the man behind me why and discover that before joining the check in queue I should have got the bag weighed. Where do I do this? He points to a man in the middle of the hall between the door and the check in desks. I never saw him when I came in, but I wasn't looking for him or his services, so I have to abandon my place in the queue and go and get my bag weighed and registered as going to Lusaka. With the bright yellow label now on my bag it is back to the check in queue where the kind passengers let me return to my previous place in the line.

Through I go to departures. At immigration it is a woman again, but not the same one as yesterday. I hand her my passport and she is flicking through all the pages. At first I don't think there is anything strange with this but when she does it again and again I begin to wonder what she is doing. I am not kept in suspense for long. She looks up over the rim of her glasses and says she can't stamp an exit visa on my passport as it doesn't have an entry visa stamped in it. What I came in yesterday! There is no record of my arrival. How could I have been so stupid not to check if I had the entry stamp? I am usually careful and check what is stamped in my passport but I think that waiting so long for someone to come and let us into the country I just forgot. How much is this going to cost me? These errors can usually be solved with some money but today I am not going to pay. I have time between now and the flight to argue my case. Why should I have to solve a problem that someone else's incompetence has created? This idea makes me smile as most problems you encounter are because someone has or hasn't done something correctly, and I am the person who wants to go through immigration. I just stand and ask what I have to do. She doesn't answer my question only repeats that she can't stamp an exit visa on a passport which doesn't have an arrival visa. Actually this I believe but it doesn't help me. She hands me back my passport and I am expecting her to tell me which office to go to when she takes my husband passport from him stamps it and returns it to him ignoring me completely. I am now on the other side of the immigration desk so I just keep walking to departures. Will anybody look again at my passport before I leave? I hope not. I can't believe what has just happened. I have been to Namibia but I haven't. No point is making a big deal of it I just hope I get out of the airport.

Breakfast time and I go to a very modern café. It is busy because it is the only one in the airport. I order a coffee and toast and cheese and sit to eat breakfast and have to listen to my husband going on and on that he can't believe that I didn't check my passport yesterday when I was given it back at immigration. Did he check his? Of course not but he never checks things like that, but I usually do. Well I didn't yesterday and I still don't know what is going to happen in the next hour so please shut up and let me eat my toast.

The departure lounge is small with some shops and the café down one side and the three or four departure gates at the other. There are no information boards. The outgoing flights are called and the passengers go to the gate announced on the loudspeaker. I must be careful. My flight going to Lusaka leaves at nine fifteen while the Luanda flight is scheduled for nine thirty-five. The voice making the announcements is not super clear so I better listen. On time again, the flight for Lusaka is announced. There would appear to be only about ten passengers. I get on the plane without having to show my passport. I sigh with relief as the Embraer lifts its nose into the air and I am on my way back to Zambia. The flight has no turbulence, breakfast is served and I sit back and reflect what happened this morning.

The flight takes one hour and fifty-five minutes and I arrive back in Zambia this time in the capital Lusaka. At the Kenneth Kaunda airport, named after the first President, the immigration officers are waiting for the flights to arrive. I have an entry visa as I got a double visa on arrival in Livingstone airport. That seems a long time ago and what a lot I have done and seen since that day. The two young men working at immigration must enjoy their jobs as every passenger is greeted with a big smile. Welcome to Zambia. They could be used in an advertising campaign by the Zambian tourist board. Just contrast them to the rude, brutish workers who "welcome" passengers to the USA. If you have ever been in Miami airport you will know what I mean. In Miami I have heard immigration officers call passengers stupid because they left one question on the immigration form blank.

The flight is five minutes early. I have been on three flights and they have all been on time. Lusaka's Kenneth Kaunda International airport is small and has a much more African feel. In Lusaka I am going to see real Africa. It is amazing that I have been in four different African countries and yet not been in real Africa. What is real Africa for me? Rundown crumbling buildings, poverty, dust, over populated spaces, street markets, peddlers and the "where have you come from" people who instantly recognise you as having just arrived.

I am staying in the Taj hotel and have booked their airport transfer at $20 each. I go outside at arrivals but there is no one to meet me so I follow the signs to the car park. In the car park there is also no Taj minivan. There is a minivan from Radisson hotel with no passengers and I ask the driver about the transport from the Taj Hotel. He tries to phone but gets no answer. A taxi driver offers to take me to the city but I explain I have reserved transport. He is very polite and hangs about in anticipation of a fare. He is in no way pushy and he is alone. Is this Africa? (I thought at the time that only one taxi waiting at the international airport was strange. Since then I have read about the murders of taxi drivers in Lusaka and other parts of Zambia in December and January, perhaps this is having an impact.) I go back into the airport just encase I missed the driver but I think that is unlikely as the arrivals is very quiet. I ask a security guard if I am in the right place and he confirms I am and says that he hasn't seen any pick up from the Taj hotel. I only reserved this a few days before I left home so they shouldn't have forgotten. I think I will go and take the blue taxi. At that point the pickup arrives, late. On this trip have used some not too well known companies and they all have been great. In Lusaka a big city where I want to be careful I am left standing at the airport by a hotel from a large five star chain. The Taj group of hotels claim that they are wonderful but this is not a good start.

But he is here now. The trip to the centre is only fourteen kilometres. Just outside the airport the land is divided into small holdings, the main industry being small scale farming. The road is obviously in Africa. There are as many people walking and riding bikes on the road as there are cars. There is no hard shoulder so people are forced onto the road with the traffic. There is a queue of cars stopped ahead at a police check point. Two blue and green chequered cars have brought the traffic to a halt. Apparently police road blocks are common here in Zambia. The driver says that the police are cracking down on drivers who have been drinking. Drinking and driving is a bit of a problem especially in the afternoon and evenings at the end of the month when people are paid. We are waved on without a second glance. A few metres on and there is brush wood on the road marking a breakdown. Although it is the law to have two warning triangles some people still don't carry them but some brush wood on the ground warns drivers that someone has a problem. Looking at the state of his car I think that he might have a big problem.

Lining both sides of this main road is land which is being farmed. In rural areas 85% of the workforce's main source of income comes from farming. The driver explains that about 100km north of Lusaka in the Provence of Kabwe the farmers are having an enormous problem with army worms. These caterpillars are wreaking havoc on agricultural crops especially the staple diet crop, maize. These worms travel in small insect armies and consume everything in their path. They are most active at night and hide under garden debris during the day. This worm which has a velvety black back, greenish yellow underside and pale stripes down its side is causing hell for many and it is spreading. The government is spraying areas and free insecticides are being given to farmers but the supply of cypermethrin which is most used is running out. The farmers now have to buy supplies themselves or wait for further supplies from the government. Small hold farmers are digging trenches around their fields in an attempt to keep their land free of this pest.

Farming provides the livelihood for the most impoverished and vulnerable people in Zambian society and I understand why this is the most talked about subject this month. The only real hope lies with the heavy rains which fall between October and March. This is the beginning of January and the invasion of these worms came in December. Army worms do not survive the rain. I hope for the farmer's the rains come soon.

The little cultivated fields are now being replaced by buildings and the road is wider. There are two lanes in both directions as we enter the city. There are lots of old cars and trucks full of people but no flash. Actually the place looks a little depressing. I soon turn into the Taj Pomodzi Hotel. At the door are standing two or three uniformed concierges complete with white hats and gloves. Very smart but the hotel looks a little tired from the outside. Inside it is deserted; there are two girls behind the reception desk. They look at me as if to ask what I am doing here. I have to wait a few minutes for the receptionist who is doing nothing to come and attend to me. This hotel is pre- paid as I reserved their Christmas offer of bed and breakfast for $145 per night. Not cheap but cheaper than the other international hotel chains. I would have preferred to stay in the new Radisson or the Protea but they were more expensive and breakfast was not included. I have no great plans for

Lusaka so a relaxing two days in my book includes a good buffet breakfast, and after all, a Taj hotel should be good enough even though I read that the standard of the Zambian Taj is nothing as good as a Taj Hotel in India.

I have to give a credit card for extras. Ok normal but it is not usual to be asked to sign a slip of paper which clearly has the name of a company on it. Could she give me another credit card slip, without someone else's name on it, to sign? The look she gives me tells me that I am truly overworking this receptionist.

The view from the room is the city of Lusaka which is great for giving me my bearings. This hotel is in the middle of nowhere but I knew that and it isn't a problem, as I will be taking a taxi most time I go out. Now I will take my book to the pool and try and catch up with some sunbathing. This is the first time on this trip that I have nothing planned to do. The pool area is quite nice, nothing special but it has the required sun loungers. There are four more people trying to improve their tan, not exactly busy. The pool is too cold for me but not for some others.

The weather is pleasant but I like it much warmer, the sky is a bit grey and I find that it is difficult to believe that I am in Africa, after all isn't Africa sunny, hot and dry? Not in Zambia in the rainy season. Although the climate is tropical Lusaka is at a height of 1,272 metres above sea level which makes its climate more pleasant than in other tropical lands. Zambia has three seasons. From December to April it is warm and wet, then from May to August it is dry and cool and in September and November it is hot and dry. With this climate Zambia can grow a range of crops including maize, tobacco, cotton, rice, wheat, sugar cane, tea and a very high quality coffee. Being tropical it produces fruit such as mangoes, avocados, pineapples, bananas and lychees.

I am soon bored with sitting here in the dull afternoon so I think it is time to go into the city centre. At the door of the hotel are a number of the blue official taxis so I ask the price to go to Cairo Road which is the main hub. I am quoted 30 kwacha. A bit expensive but that is what you get when you take a taxi from a hotel door. It isn't far. It is Saturday afternoon, the banks and big businesses are closed so I am not expecting to see Cairo Road at its most active.

I asked the taxi driver to drop me at Shop rite store but now I am here I am not so sure I want to stay. This city centre is depressing. Cairo Road is one long straight street going through the middle of the city. With the shops shut this main artery doesn't look like somewhere I want to walk. I do some quick thinking and negotiate with the taxi driver to take me a round of the centre and back to the hotel. For another 20 kwacha I can see of the centre without tiring myself out. There are few people around and those who are hanging about are men. On the pavements are street traders trying to sell mainly shoes. There are great piles of them displayed on the ground. They are not doing much business mainly due to the lack of passing trade. In a city of two million I expected to see more activity even on a Saturday afternoon. Outside Protea Hotel Cairo road are two men with shirts for sale. These are propped in a line along the front of the hotel. I suppose that is very handy for a businessman who arrives in the city without his luggage. He can buy a shirt on the pavement while staying in this business hotel.

I am heading north to the area near the bus station and my surroundings are getting shoddier. I wonder how different I would have found this city if I had arrived by bus from Victoria Falls. This was one of the options I considered at the planning stage because a flight from Victoria Falls to Lusaka is expensive. Perhaps this is because there seems to be only one company flying this route so Proflight can set its own fares. If I hadn't gone to Namibia I would have taken the bus from Victoria Falls to Lusaka. The Mazhandu Family bus company run reliable daily services which take about seven hours. I seriously considered doing this and staying in the Protea Hotel here in Cairo Road in the heart of the city. Instead I am in a five star hotel in the middle of nowhere with a nice pool which is too cold to swim in. I am really doubting my choice of hotel as I like to be in the heart of things.

My city tour didn't take long. That is because there isn't much to see in Lusaka. It is not a must see city mainly a means to an end. From here you can visit many interesting game parks and cultural villages. Zambia is not lacking in things to do or see and many are less than an hour from the city. I have two days here in the city and I investigated what I could do with the time and the truth is not much as I don't want to go to a national park or see more animals. The taxi driver offers to take me around tomorrow, so I ask what I will see. He could take me to the Sunday craft market. Great, that is my plan for tomorrow. Does he have any more ideas about what I should see? No, so my research was right. Lusaka hasn't much to visit but it is a great gateway to many wonderful truly African sights. I have on this adventure been to Chobe National Park, explored the wilderness of Botswana so I am personally ready for some African city life.

One place I looked at when thinking about what I could do here was Chaminuka Game Park. On their web site it looks great. It is set in 10,000 acres of pristine miobo woodland and savannah and is home to lions, hyena, elephants, giraffes, zebra and others, some seventy-two species of Zambian bush animals and birds. It offers game drives, bush walks, fishing and horseback safaris and the greatest thing is that it is only twenty minutes from the airport or forty from the city centre, but note that the road to this lodge isn't great. This place has been up and running since the1970's and is not just a game reserve but a whole community of three villages, two school, a church, a clinic, a pig farm and the Kaposhi cheese factory. If you want to experience rural Zambia while in Lusaka and don't want to travel far from the capital this lodge seems an interesting option although the price like all private game parks is not cheap. I haven't gone to Chaminuka because as I said I want o be in the city and I have seen enough wild life on this trip.

Back at the Taj Pomodzi and I pay the taxi driver the agreed fifty kwacha. He attempts to pin me down on a time to go to the Sunday market tomorrow but I don't really know when I will want to go so that is a fare he won't get. As you will have gathered from reading that every day on this trip was full of adventure so the time in Lusaka doesn't have to be so action packed. My idea is to see another African city and enjoy the good weather before returning to the winter weather in Europe.

I am a little disappointed that I didn't find a book shop in Lusaka. I want to buy a copy of "Dead Aid" by Dambisa Moyo the international economist. "Dead Aid" is on the New York Times bestsellers list. This well educated African woman grew up in Lusaka so I would have liked to buy the book in her home city. Moyo delivers a message of political incorrectness, one I agree with totally. She states that aid to Africa should be cut. She argues that aid has not merely failed to work but has compounded Africa's problem. She highlights the sharp contrast between countries that rejected the aid route and prospered with countries which are aid dependent and have seen poverty increase. She compares aid to oil. It enables the powerful elite to embezzle public revenues. Aid is easy money. If a government had to rely upon private finance they would become accountable to the lenders and if they had to rely on taxation they would be accountable to the voters. Unlike Moyo I am neither a Harwood nor Oxford graduate nor a consultant at the World Bank in Washington but I have always questioned the value the aid. Does Africa need more Moyo and less Bono? If she is right it may be time to turn off the aid tap. Having travelled the world, seen some of the poorest areas, visited some rather primitive regions and met many different nationalities, I have questioned the value of hand outs for many years. I am not suggesting we just abandon countries that are in need of help but rethink what we can do which is constructive in improving their lot. For me this book is a must read but I will have to wait till I get home.

This five star Taj Hotel is a little spooky. There are no less than three white capped, very smartly dressed doormen welcoming me back to the hotel. Inside is like a ghost town, there's all this space for me. The foyer is beautiful with big comfy leather sofas, crystal chandeliers and a grand piano. All it needs are some guests. Up I go to the room, of course not meeting any other clients in the lift or corridors. I open the door and walk in to find the carpet and bed covered in rose petals and all the lamps have big white bows tied to them. Do they think I have just got married? I kick off my shoes only to find that when I walk about the soles of my feet are sticking to these floral displays. Never mind before I went out I put some drinks in the mini bar so the water should be nice and cool. Great! The contents of the fridge are warm; it doesn't seem to be functioning well. Next to the bathroom where I have no small towels only bath towels. That is fantastic; beside the wash hand basin is a box which says it contains a tooth brush, this is just what I am needing, a clean brush. I open the box and out pops one of these mini tubes of toothpaste but no brush. I am feeling a little confused by the service here but on the coffee table there is a bowl of fruit, that's nice. Well it would be if there was a plate and knife to eat it with. I don't like to sound as if I am complaining but I think I am beginning to understand why the hotel is short of guests, after all it is not the only five star hotel here in Lusaka. I am paying $145 a night, bed and breakfast, Christmas special, which is a fantastically low price as this hotel usually charges over $200, but I think that I would prefer to have a towel than these stupid petals which are driving me crazy. When they are on a tiled floor they just seem to get lost but here on the carpet they are a pest.

I have mentioned some small niggles concerning this hotel but I have to say that the dinner was very good. One thing that never fails to surprise me is the good quality of hotel food served in Africa. Perhaps this is because I am British but live in Spain, so my normal daily diet is Mediterranean. Here in Africa the food has a British twist to it, which I enjoy. On this continent I have enjoyed dinners which reminded me of Christmas dinners back home, meat pies and other British fare, like tonight in this hotel with classic fish and chips.

The night life here in Lusaka is not for me so again it is early to bed. My biological clock is now tuned to rising early and being a sleep by ten. Today has been very low keyed. Saturday wasn't the best day to see Lusaka, one of the fastest growing cities in Africa.

Day 6

Oh good a newspaper under the door. I would never buy a newspaper on holiday but I really enjoy it when one is pushed under the bedroom door for me to read. I like to read about what is going on in the country. Right, what is in The Lusaka Times today? The usual articles discussing politicians and their different degrees of questionable honesty. Not too appealing a read, but now this looks interesting, an article about a Livingstone man who had stolen some chickens. Apparently he was caught red handed and tried to escape but was chased by some people. In an attempt to escape capture he dived into the Zambezi River where he was attacked by a crocodile which bit off his hand. That really is rough justice.

Another article which I find amusing is about a woman who was taken before a judge because her husband felt that his wife was disrespectful because when she served chicken she took the best parts for herself and gave the less meaty bits to her husband. The outcome of this trial is also intriguing as the judge declared that the said woman was indeed badly brought up and that the blame lay with her mother for not teaching her how to look after a husband correctly. Oh a great little story and an insight into village life.

The other story which catches my eye is about the new money. Some people in the villages are finding the new notes confusing and some unscrupulous beings are cheating them out of their hard earned cash. In a foreign country you tend to be on the lookout for being overcharged or being given the wrong change but in reality crooks take advantage of anyone. No time to finish reading the newspaper as my husband has surfaced and is demanding his breakfast.

Breakfast in the large airy dining room overlooking the gardens is very relaxing. Every breakfast so far on this trip has been followed by packing my bag and hitting the road. This is the first breakfast that I haven't had one eye on my watch. I can sit here and really enjoy Sunday breakfast. It is also very nice that there is only one more person in the restaurant. One big disadvantage of holidaying in a business hotel is that while you are trying to disconnect others around you are engaged in business chatter with colleagues or even worse shouting down a mobile phone. Thankfully this is not happening here. The only interruption to my thoughts is an over attentive waiter hovering around at my elbow. In spite of his presence I am going to take a bun in the plastic bag in my bag for my mid-morning coffee. If not, where am I going to find a baker's here in Lusaka. I have found many small imperfections in this hotel but I can't criticize the breakfast buffet.

The rose petals are now beginning to wilt a little as I pad around packing my little day rucksack for my visit to the Sunday craft market in the car park at the Arcades shopping centre. Will I take my umbrella? Although it is the rainy season and I have been expecting to get caught in a typical African rain storm I have so far avoided it. I am still covering myself in Deet as mosquitos are still a potential danger.

I know where I am going because I passed both Arcades and Manda Hill shopping centres on the way from the airport to the hotel yesterday. Again I take a taxi from inside the grounds of the hotel. I agree to the fare of 35 kwacha. Here in Lusaka there is no mention of dollars everything is in the local currency. The trip to Arcades takes about five minutes and I am dropped off in the car park where the Pakati market is. Half of the car park is occupied by the market and parked around are taxis and cars. The taxi driver wants to wait for me but I don't want to be tied down to a pre arranged time. Looking around I won't have a problem getting a taxi for the return trip. Now where will I start? On first glance I think I will be here for some time. Many of the goods for sale are displayed on the ground but there are some market stalls. I think I will firstly just walk around and look at everything. The traders are friendly and a little insistent that I look at their goods, after all in a country where 60% of the population are unemployed and making a living is a task; would you not try very hard to separate a European visitor from her kwacha?

Pakati market

Paintings for sale Pakati market

The paintings are incredible. I can imagine some of them adorning a wall in my house. Here in the market they are lying on the ground in rows of four eight painting deep. They all have the same theme but are very different and choosing one will be difficult. They have such bright hues with the predominate colours being red, orange and black. The designs are very African and the paintings are mostly of elephants, other animals, maps of Africa and rondavels. I stop and admire some and the seller is quite pushy but I am comfortable in a market like this. I know what I want to buy and I won't be influenced by determined salesmen.

I walk on a little and am invited by a polite, pretty woman of about twenty years old to look at her wooden bowls. They are all sizes and made from brown and black coloured wood. They, like the paintings are all arranged on the ground. I promise to come back and buy something from her.

Little metal bikes

As well as the usual crafts of wooden animals and masks there are some more original items. One man is selling ornaments which are little bikes made of metal and they are being ridden by little figures made of ceramic all wearing colourful shirts or dresses made from the same material. Each rider is carrying something on his or her bike. Some have logs and others are transporting woven baskets. They really are different and well made. The problem with things like these is that they look good here but when you take them home they look a bit shabby. For sale next to these ornaments are items which are more difficult to transport, but they are good. My grandson would be delighted if I arrived back home with one of these metre and a half tall drums.

Jade, Jade, Jade

Jade. It is everywhere, this beautiful green brightening the whole market. There are great lumps of it; it is made into bracelets, elephants and even draught sets. Jade is not the only semi precious stone for sale here, there is also stones of amber and blue and white, a reminder that Zambia has a wealth of precious stones including emeralds, aquamarines and amethysts. For the lovers of bead jewellery this is heaven. Necklaces, earrings and bracelets hang in great bundles of colour.

Bead zebras

Now these, laid out on newspaper on the ground, are an original use of beads. Bead zebras, little animals made from black and white glass beads with a metal frame. How cute, great presents for little girls.

More paintings

No trader is aggressively pushy except one man who seems to pop up every time I turn a corner. He has no stall or pitch and is carrying his wares around. He is selling copper bracelets and I am limping slightly so I think he has marked me as someone who could benefit from his product. About four or five times he comes between me and what I am trying to see and I have had enough of him so it is time to explain firmly that one hundred per cent I will not be buying a copper bracelet, so he has to stop harassing me and go and find another potential client as he is wasting his time and I am getting ratty. It is not surprising to see copper bracelets here, as Zambia has 6% of the worlds copper reserves and is the fourth largest copper producer in the world. When I think about it I am surprised not to see more items made of copper for sale. Perhaps this is because the Chinese seem have a lot of control of the copper mines. This was certainly the opinion of one man I spoke to. He was of the opinion that the Chinese have taken the place of the Europeans in milking Zambia of its riches.

I have now walked round all the stalls so it is time to think about what I am going to buy. I could buy so many things. When I was younger I would buy loads of things in a market like this and then arrive home and wonder where I was going to put my purchases and many have spent their entire life in a box in a cupboard. Because many of these items have been bought in places I will never visit again I am reluctant to bin them, so, each time I have a clean out they go back in the same place in the box. Now I am older I am much more selective about what I buy. That doesn't mean that I don't buy crazy things that my patient husband has to carry home. On a trip to Dakar I bought a fairly large wooden elephant weighing about eleven kilos who has pride of place on the stairs in my house, so what am I going to buy here in Lusaka? Right now nothing as I am going to go into Arcades shopping centre.

Arcades is actually a small but modern mall on one level. It has some nice eating places including places offering pizza and pasta, and for anyone pinning for fast food there is a Wimpy and a Subway. It seems to have a proliferation of mobile phone outlets competing in number with banks. But I am looking for internet to catch up with my emails. Next to the dry cleaners I find what I am looking for and much cheaper than in the hotel.

On my left is the door to the casino in the Protea hotel which is actually in the centre and I would love to be staying here instead of in the Taj which is in the middle of nowhere. So why am I staying in a hotel which isn't my first choice? Two reasons, firstly price. Because of the Xmas special the Taj was about sixty dollars a night cheaper and I reckoned for the hundred and twenty dollars difference I could take a few taxis and still be in pocket. Secondly snobbery. I have never before stayed in a Taj hotel. The two hotels here in the area of Arcades are the new Radisson Blue and the Protea. I have stayed in these chains before and although I would definitely prefer to stay here I could not justify the price difference and miss out on a Taj experience.

I am not going to spend much time inside the centre as it is not what I came here to see but I am going to pay a visit to the Spar supermarket and buy some fruit for lunch. With the exception of the heavily armoured guard patrolling the isles with an AK 47 riffle, this Spar could be in any British town.

With my groceries safely packed away in my small rucksack on my back I am again off to the market outside, this time with the intention to buy. I have decided to be selective and only purchase some wooden bowls and a painting. I am tempted to buy some of the beautiful African printed material which is hanging all around me but what would I do with it when I get home? I know the answer. I will put it in the cupboard with the material I bought in Madagascar, so why buy it? Oh look at these stools. They have three bamboo legs and a skin seat on which is painted the face of a lion or a giraffe. I know a few children who would love one of these but how on earth could I carry them without damaging them. I walk down the aisle between the traders sitting on the ground with their wares and wish I could buy something from everyone as some of them must have spent hours making what they are trying to sell. I have not been hassled or pressured into buying but I have heard lots of stories about if people like me, don't buy things, the workers won't have money to buy food for their children.

Bamboo and leather stools

As I approach the stall selling the wooden bowls the pretty girl hands me the bowl I had been looking at. Now I just have to get the price down to what I want to pay. After a few minutes she wraps my two bowls up in newspaper. They are really pretty, black and brown and not too heavy or awkward to carry. My next visit is the stall selling paintings. Like the stall selling the bowls it is one of many with the same items for sale but I have said that I would come back to these stalls and buy. Choosing a painting is proving much more difficult. I like about six of them and no, I am not buying half a dozen. Finally I decide on one in black and dark orangey red about 90x60 cms in size. It is a map of Africa with Zambia coloured black and on the right a black baobab tree with a black elephant on the left and four rondavels covering the north of the continent. I think it is very representative of this trip. My husband insists on carrying it as I have a reputation for scrunching everything into my bag.

There are now one or two tourists looking around, some with guides. I can't imagine going round a market with a guide at my tail. It would be horrible for me but would make a guide quite dizzy as I weave my way around sometimes to the left or right or back the way I have just come. It would take a good guide to follow me around. Actually my husband and I have an agreement that if we get separated we look for each other for about half an hour and if during that time we haven't found each other we go back to the hotel, hopefully to be reunited. We have never had to put this plan into practice, but agreed on it after being in a night market in Hong Kong where if we had got separated we would never have found each other until the market closed and the hundreds of shoppers had gone home. Losing each other here is not likely to happen as there are so few people and the area is small. I could spend hours here but my husband has had enough African crafts, so it is time to go back to the hotel. Finding a taxi is easy. Actually they are coming towards me as I leave the stalls. Thirty kwacha to go back to the hotel. This is about five dollars. Like I said, I can take a few taxis for the price difference between the hotel I am in and the one I wanted to be in. Perhaps it is a blessing that I am not staying in a hotel overlooking the market as I would surely pop out and go crazy buying things.

The old taxi driver needs to buy petrol before we can go anywhere. This he can do in the car park where there are some petrol pumps. At least he doesn't ask to be paid before the journey but he waited to get some business before filling the tank with petrol. In India and Asia I have often been asked by the taxi driver for money to buy petrol on route with the amount spent on fuel taken off the agreed taxi fare at the end of the trip. I don't in any way feel this is wrong but this Zambian taxi driver has money for his petrol.

Back in the hotel and it is time to relax by the pool. The weather on this trip has not been at all like I expected it to be. I thought it would be very hot with thunderstorms but it is not hot and I have had very little rain but today the sky is grey. My trip to four neighbouring countries in Africa is over. Early tomorrow morning I fly back to London. It has been very enjoyable and like the weather very different from how I imagined it would be. This has been an easy to do trip and for anyone who is a little apprehensive about tackling Africa independently this could be for you.

My previous experiences in Africa have consisted of overcrowded run-down streets, where walking around attracted a lot of unwelcome attention. And then the killer, public transport mini buses, which race each other to their destination and although they were designed to take eight people have about eighteen travellers squashed in and a tout still finding space for one more. I have driven open roads where drivers are advised not to stop as carjacks are likely to happen. I have had a guide in taxi demand money on the way from an airport to the city late at night and threaten If I didn't pay him extra he would make the taxi driver stop and put me out of the vehicle in the dark in the middle of nowhere. These are just some of my less enjoyable moments associated with travel in Africa so why has this been so smooth? There are a number of reasons.

Firstly I have not travelled on public transport. The distances are were short and private transfers are not expensive so I have used this method, plus flights, to get about saving me the hassle of bus stations in poorer parts of towns such as in Lusaka. My preferred mode of travel is by train as it brings you into direct contact with the local people but here in this part of Africa the trains, where they had them, have now gone. The truth is that to travel the route I have just done on public transport is nearly impossible. The longest road trip was from Victoria Falls town Zimbabwe to Kazungula on the frontier of Botswana which was on a well tarred road with little traffic. It was a strange journey for me because my previous experiences of African roads have been of rutted highways and vehicles which were by their sell by date, people walking in the middle of the road carrying a variety goods and the lucky ones with bicycles all weaving in and out of each other and of course, the occasional animal. This road on the other hand was ghostly under-used, a clinical unmemorable drive, it sure didn't feel like the other Africa I had visited.

Jumping from one country to another has incurred a number of land border crossings. The internet is full of horror stories about the difficulties people had encountered at these points. I can say that I had no problems with getting visas quickly and efficiently, my only problem was in Windhoek airport which should have been the easiest.

On the subject of transport the three short flights, one with Air Botswana and two with Air Namibia, were on time with the planes and service good. My planned route was tightly organised with very little margin for no-show or late flights but I never needed the alternative plans.

Secondly I have not arrived anywhere after dark. When the sun set I have been safely installed in a hotel. I have also chosen top quality hotels with the security that comes with them. Even having a safe deposited box to store your valuables, such as passport and visa cards, in while out and about can take the pressure off. I now seldom stay in cheap accommodation. I have found that often it is more economical to stay in a nice hotel with a room where I am happy to spend some time, perhaps doing as I did today, bringing in fruit and a snack for lunch saving me from having to buy lunch in a restaurant. If I am being careful with money it is often cheaper to stay in a good hotel with a comfortable room, bring in a snack for lunch and a takeaway or something from a supermarket for dinner, than to stay in a cheap hotel where I have to spend money just to pass the time getting away from the not so nice room. On any trip it is the food and bar costs that very quickly mount up. I have eaten many "room service" dinners accompanied by a bottle of wine from a supermarket therefore halving the cost of eating.

Number three, which perhaps should have been number one if I were putting these in order of importance, was the professional attitude of the local people who are in the tourist trade. This became obvious to me from the beginning when I started emailing people about hotels and road transfers. The replies were swift in coming back and often contained extra useful information that I had not asked for. On the ground the high quality of service was recommendable from drivers to waiters. The tourist trade is a big money earner and in this part of Africa it has huge potential. If the majority of people involved are similar to the people I dealt with it will have a rosy future.

In Zimbabwe I only visited the town of Victoria falls, in Zambia Livingston and the capital Lusaka, in Botswana Maun and Kasane and in Namibia the capital Windhoek so I have only had an introduction to these countries. It would take months to explore these countries fully but as a visitor to any country it is a special treat if you can "do" the complete country in one visit. Let's be honest, I am a world traveller and I have not visited everywhere in my native Scotland, but I know the land well. Although my visit here has been short I am leaving with a very positive attitude to the people from this part of the world. It seems to

me that the new attitude from the modern Africa is predominant in the people here. They want to be part of the modern world and be seen as a success, not as part of the continent that expects to live on hand outs from the wealthier west. I have enjoyed meeting the proud folks from these parts.

Tomorrow is another early rise. The BA flight departs at nine so I will have to be out of the hotel just after six. I switch off the light and as my head hits the pillow for my last night in Africa I wonder what if anything would have made this trip better. This is always a question I put to myself at this point and this time I know the answer. I would have liked another day in Livingston at the very beginning of my visit, not to see more of the Victoria Falls just to see the town and have time to visit the children at the orphanage. Then why did I not organise this if that was what I wanted to do? Simple, I had no choice in the BA flight from London to Livingston. To get the cheap price I had to fly on New Year's Eve, and then the Air Botswana flight to Maun only goes two days a week so I had to be in Kasane two days later to catch the flight to Maun. The number of days in each place was determined by the flights, but it all worked out just perfectly.

Good Bye Africa

It is 6am and I am again sitting in the dining room of the Taj hotel. This hotel gets top marks for opening up to give British Airways passengers breakfast before they leave. Breakfast is not as relaxed as yesterday but I am delighted with the service given by the hotel and it would appear that I am the only guest having breakfast at this early hour.

The minivan doing the transfer to Kenneth Kaunda Airport is now leaving the grounds of the Taj Hotel with only us. Where are the people? I know that the flight to London is full so I would expect some other travelling companions. The drive out of Lusaka is on a dual carriageway and the city is wakening up. This road is crazy. Drivers can turn right onto the other side of the dual carriageway but there is no lane to do this so the cars turning right are stopped in the fast lane of the left hand side waiting for a break in the traffic to join the flow in the opposite direction. Driving along here I am constantly reminded by signs that the transport system here benefited from aid from Japan.

Kenneth Kaunda airport is very busy, the majority of passengers being for the London flight. Upstairs in the departure lounge there is a café and a small well stocked souvenir shop where I buy a mouse pad of Zambia. There are no monitors and the departure procedure a little confusing. In the queue for boarding the London flight are a few passengers who are actually going to Johannesburg but attentive staff are on hand to smooth over these hiccups. A bus takes the economy passengers to the steps of the plane driving past the business passengers who are having to walk. Can't work out the logic in this move but I am certainly not complaining.

No time wasted and the flight, which has not one empty seat, is up in the air heading north to Europe. Airlines all round the world appear to be in financial difficulties but every time I get on a flight it is full. I would really like to ask my fellow passengers where they have come from. What were they all doing in the Lusaka area or were they like me and came from other parts of Southern Africa? Lusaka is a wonder point to begin an adventure. The country of Zambia is 752,000sq kms, about the combined size of France, Belgium, Holland and Switzerland. For the traveller it has a rich variety of activities. It has many game parks and lodges, where animal viewing is spectacular. The most popular of these are South Luangwa and Lower Zambezi but some like Kafue are only a two hour drive from both Lusaka and Livingstone. The main season for the game parks is from April to November and in the Emerald season not all are open. Whether a lodge or park is open all year or not is often related to the terrain. Some roads become inaccessible in the rainy season.

The two main reasons tourists visit Zambia are to go on safari to experience the bush, and see animals and visit the Victoria Falls but I was surprised at the number of activities that were on offer in Livingstone. For me I came only to see the Falls, but the tourists here can do a number of activities. You can go on an elephant back safari, do walks with lions and cheetahs and the adventure sports will surely get the adrenalin flowing. If I was ever tempted to do bungee jumping the place to do it must be from the Bridge into the Batoka Gorge. If bungee jumping isn't your thing then perhaps abseiling or white water rafting is. All of these can be reserved through companies in Victoria Falls or Livingstone but the

company I used and found to be very helpful was Adventurezone in Victoria Falls. There are enough things to do around the falls to keep you busy for a good few days.

Zambia is a wonderful country with wonderful people just waiting for a visit from you. If you are like me and want to notch up a few more countries visited, what could be a better base than landlocked Zambia surrounded by no less than eight countries. You have a choice of adding on some of its neighbours as I did. Zambia surely is the heart of Africa surrounded by The Congo, Tanzania, Malawi, Angola, Mozambique, Zimbabwe, Botswana and Namibia. It's no wonder that the plane is full.

I wonder if any of my fellow travellers, if they came from London to Lusaka, were involved in the Red Cross project of bringing a manually operated sewing machine to Zambia. Travellers from Heathrow are wanted to take sewing machines as part of their luggage. It does not affect your luggage allowance as BA transports the machines free. All you are doing is chaperoning the machine on its trip. If you agree to participate in this scheme you are met in Heathrow and given the machines by a Red Cross member. After check-in, BA takes it to Lusaka where you are met by a person from the Red Cross there, who takes possession of it. The Red Cross, who started this scheme in February 2010, have already delivered 300 cases of these machines to people in the country who are now able to make a living mending garments or even starting a simple tailoring business. Owning a basic sewing machine can turn around a poor person's life, giving him or her means to earn enough money for food and medicine. This project has been so successful in Zambia that the Red Cross are now extending it to Kenya, so if you are travelling to Lusaka or Nairobi you too can help. Contact the Red Cross at least a month before you travel and do your bit for Africa.

For the second time today I am having breakfast and inwardly reminiscing about the things I have seen and the people that I have met. It is to me an enigma that a country with such a wealth in gems and minerals, a climate suitable for producing food for all its citizens and neighbours, a healthy tourist industry with so much to offer and a population prepared to work, should need aid which ranges from the great funds poured in from Japan and China to the sewing machines supplied by the Red Cross.

Will I ever understand Africa? I doubt it but it is great fun trying. I hope I can return one day soon.

Printed in Great Britain
by Amazon